5.00

# Modern Airweapon Shooting

# Modern Airweapon Shooting

**Bob Churchill & Granville Davies**

Drawings by Ann Churchill

DAVID & CHARLES

Newton Abbot    London    North Pomfret (Vt)

**British Library Cataloguing in Publication Data**

Churchill, Bob
  Modern airweapon shooting.
  1. Air guns
  2. Shooting
  I. Title     II. Davies, Granville
  799.3′12       GV1174

  ISBN 0–7153–8123–7

Typeset by Typesetters (Birmingham) Limited,
Smethwick, Warley, West Midlands
and printed in Great Britain
by Redwood Burn Limited, Trowbridge, Wiltshire
for David & Charles (Publishers) Limited
Brunel House  Newton Abbot  Devon

# Contents

# PART 1

# 1 An Introduction to Airweapon Shooting

The modern airweapon is simply a sophisticated version of a very old and primitive weapon – the blowpipe. In its most basic form, a blowgun need only be a hollow reed through which the gunner, using lung power alone, blows a small missile such as a pebble or dart. A modern version of the simple reed pipe is the pea-shooter, a familiar children's toy, which, in common with the blowpipe of the American Indians and the most advanced of today's target airweapons, employs a principle as old as man. Indeed, the ability of air under pressure to propel a missile has been known in all civilisations, and the airweapon can be fairly considered as the ancestor of every firearm, from lady's handbag pistol to 17in naval cannon

## The Blowpipe

No doubt at some time in the very misty past, on the bank of some forgotten lake, a man idly toying with a hollow reed realised that he could, by blowing down one end shoot a small missile from the other. The nearby lakeshore would provide suitable bullets – pebbles perhaps, a sliver of wood, or a thorn from an overhanging tree. A bird in the same tree would have been a tempting target to try out the weapons on, and in a very short time the new toy would have become an important provider of food. In the fifteenth century the blowpipe was used for hunting even in Europe, so it is safe to assume that it was widely known elsewhere.

The centuries saw little change in the construction of the pipe itself, but the missiles were many and varied. Early civilisations used hollow clay balls which broke apart on impact to discharge Greek fire — a type of incendiary material. This device finds its modern counterpart in glass ampoules filled with phosphorus, fired by saboteurs into fields of grain to burn crops. But these missiles were somewhat out of the main stream, and in any event, must have been fairly dangerous to the gunner using them. A more common development was the use of deadly poisons on darts; the Indians of South America extracting curare from a toxic plant, while Africans preferred a distillate from a tree bark. By all accounts these poisons are deadly, and significantly increase the killing efficiency of what is basically a low-powered weapon.

Man has always been able to find a war-like application for his inventions, but the blowpipe, while being no exception, has always been a fringe weapon of war. In emergencies lethal weapons have been made from domestic water pipes, hollow walking sticks and the like.

One might be excused for thinking that the rightful place in the twentieth century for a blowpipe is in a museum, but the device is still in common use in many parts of the world. Apart from the important business of providing food — a prime function in Africa or South America — the blowpipe has also been used by ornithologists wishing to collect birds without damaging their plumage.

The basic material of a blowpipe varies from country to country, depending on local availability, and in the Amazon basin is typically a reed encased in a palm sleeve. The finished blowpipe, complete with rodent tooth sights, is about 11ft long, ½in in diameter and weighs about 1lb. The darts, made from the ribs of palm leaves, air sealed with a tuft of wild cotton, leave the pipe with a velocity of 310ft/sec, comparing favourably with modern airweapons.

### Airweapons

In the sense that airweapons use the expansion of air to fire projectiles, they are merely a modern development of the ancient blowpipe, but there is an important difference. The

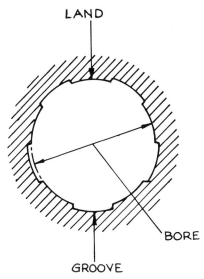

LAND

BORE

GROOVE

1 Cross section of a rifled barrel

airweapon uses not human lung power but the much greater energy stored in a highly compressed gas, usually air, thus giving higher muzzle velocities in much smaller, more convenient weapons.

There tends to be a deal of confusion over the use of the terms 'gun' and 'rifle', and since they both have quite specific meanings in shooting parlance, it is worth defining them. A gun is a weapon having a smooth bore; that is to say, the interior of the barrel is smooth along its entire length. A rifle, on the other hand is a weapon having a 'rifled' or spiral-grooved bore. The grooves cause the bullet to spin in flight, and this makes it more accurate. The 'calibre' or 'bore' of a weapon with a rifled barrel is given by an internal measurement, from one of the 'lands' across the barrel to the opposing 'groove' (Fig 1). It would be convenient, but no doubt too simple if the terms 'gun' and 'rifle' were always applied as descriptions of a weapon's barrel design, but over the years some oddities of usage have slipped in. For example, an artillery piece is called a 'field gun', but invariably has a rifled barrel, while 'hand-gun' means pistol but again a rifled barrel is normal. The word 'rifle', used as a noun, means a weapon designed to be fired from the shoulder, using both hands. The list is extensive and confusing, but as far as airweapons are concerned, the following are the accepted meanings of the terms:

**An air rifle** is a compressed gas weapon having a rifled barrel and designed to be fired from the shoulder, using both hands. Usually an air rifle is used to fire lead pellets of various designs, including spherical balls. Pointed darts and shot charges are used only by the foolhardy, as they damage the rifling.

**An air pistol** is a compressed gas weapon, having either a smooth or rifled bore, and designed to be fired from one hand. Early air pistols, particularly those intended for children, were built with smooth bores for short-range indoor shooting with feathered darts. Great accuracy was not a strong point of these weapons, and in recent years, as precision shooting became an obsession among competition marksmen, pistols with rifled barrels have become universal.

## Systems of Propulsion

### SPRING COMPRESSION

This type of airweapon is the most common, and works on the 'bicycle pump' principle. When the weapon is cocked a spring is compressed and held by the trigger mechanism. On firing, the spring is released, and as it uncoils, it drives an attached piston down a close-fitting tube. The air thus compressed is forced through a narrow vent at the end of the tube and behind the pellet, the latter being forced rapidly down the barrel by the explosive build up of pressure. Clearly a great deal of mechanical activity takes place in a short space of time, and therein lies the greatest potential problem of spring compression airweapons: a considerable amount of vibration for the shooter to cope with. Modern target weapons have compensating devices for suppressing the vibration and are essential for serious target shooting.

## PNEUMATIC PROPULSION

This type of weapon relies upon the air being compressed before firing, usually during the cocking procedure. The high-pressure air is stored in a chamber, to be released at the moment of firing. Clearly this eliminates any vibration, as the only mechanical movement during firing is that of the trigger action and pellet; no springs and pistons hurtling backwards and forwards to upset the weapon's balance. On the debit side is the necessity to 'pump' up the weapon before firing. This can mean operating a very stiff lever, not too much of a problem with a rifle, but often a tiresome chore with a pistol. A secondary problem can be the seals on the pressure chamber. Since the air pressure must be identical from shot to shot fired over many years, regardless of the time spent in the aim, a pneumatic weapon must be of the very finest construction. Generally such rifles and pistols are more expensive than spring compression weapons.

## COMPRESSED GAS PROPULSION

An obvious solution to the problem of airweapon propellants is to have the pressure vessel external to the gun − a cylinder or sphere previously charged with a gas under pressure, simply attached to the weapon before firing. Early inventors used cylinders of compressed air releasing a small amount of air for each shot, but this has the considerable disadvantage of giving a slightly reduced charge each time the gun is fired. To the marksman this means altering the sights between each shot, an impossible burden. The answer was found in the physical properties of liquid carbon dioxide. Unlike compressed air, $CO_2$ will maintain a constant pressure of gas over liquid throughout its working life. Modern $CO_2$ guns use the small cylinders sold to charge soda-water syphons as their propellant, and such weapons are convenient and accurate in use, if rather expensive to run. An additional disadvantage is the requirement, in Britain, that owners of $CO_2$ weapons must hold a Firearm Certificate.

## History of Airweapons

Although the first reliable description of a mechanical airgun dates only from the sixteenth century, it seems reasonable to assume that since the Greeks understood the principle of the syringe, some form of now forgotten airweapon could well have been developed in the pre-Christian era.

Over the centuries air power was used in a bewildering variety of weapons, many intended primarily for killing. Early European airweapons differed little externally from the firearms of the day. One preserved weapon is of flintlock pattern, and although complete with hammer and flashpan, nevertheless discharged its bullets by release of compressed air, stored either in the gun butt, or in an external flask (Fig 2).

For a brief period, during the Napoleonic Wars, air rifles saw service in French hands against the Austrians. The weapon used, a repeating rifle, was first built secretly in 1780, and fired a bullet nearly ½in in diameter with great effect at ranges up to 100yd. The Austrian troops were appalled by the silent death it brought, and killed without mercy any French soldiers they found carrying an air rifle. This, coupled with a shortage of the skilled riflesmiths needed to keep the air rifle in action, ended the use of the airgun as a service weapon.

Although the airgun was used only briefly as a weapon of war, it saw rather more service as a hunting weapon. Modern airweapons are only suitable for killing ground game and vermin, but earlier weapons, being more powerful, were used for hunting royal game. Louis XV was one of many royal persons who hunted stag and wild boar with an air rifle, and it is recorded that in 1747 he took a 480lb stag with twenty-two point antlers using an air rifle. Such a rifle would have fired a very large bullet, probably of .50 calibre, propelled by

2 'Flintlock' large calibre air rifle, with external air reservoir

a charge of air at a pressure of around 1000lb/sq in. Later, in the nineteenth century, Lewis and Clark carried a large bore air rifle with them on their celebrated expedition, but as firearms became more reliable and accurate, the airweapon returned to the role for which it is best suited, that of amusement and friendly competition. In America the development of small calibre airweapons came about by chance. In 1888, Clarence Hamilton, an inventor, showed an air rifle he had made to an industrialist, a Mr L. C. Hough, the owner of a company that made agricultural windmills. Mr Hough is said to have exclaimed 'It's a daisy!', and decided, as a gimmick, to give one away free to every farmer who purchased a windmill. Within a year the company had ceased windmill production and was making instead 'Daisy' air rifles by the hundred. The Daisy company is still producing air rifles and pistols, and has probably manufactured more airweapons than all other makers put together.

In Britain the manufacture of airweapons was in the hands of two Midlands' companies – BSA and Webley & Scott. Both were world famous for their cartridge firearms, and so airweapons manufacture was at first only a sideline. Demand grew and both companies expanded their airweapons division to such an extent that they reached a dominant position over the British market. However, continental gunmakers had been developing their own airweapons, and it fell to a German gunmaker to produce the first recoilless target air rifle. This was a major step forward, and led to the development of the sport to world championship status, and, it is expected, inclusion in the Olympics of 1984. While British airweapon manufacturers have not kept up with modern design trends, British shooters are among the world's best in a sport that is being recognised as one of the more difficult of the shooting disciplines.

## The Airweapon Today

What an airweapon lacks in power, it more than compensates for in short-range accuracy. Modern competition air rifles and pistols are capable of hitting a 1mm Bull at 10m, the international competition distance, and this represents a consistent error considerably less than even the finest marksmen can usually achieve. That the airweapon has come of age is reflected in the variety of competitions open to marksmen – from club level, through county to national, European and world championship. A competition quality weapon is expensive, but once acquired is cheap and, above all, convenient to use. An airweapon, unlike a firearm, does not require a special police approved firing range; any garden with a convenient wall is a ready made practise range.

The ready availability and wide variety of airweapons in sports shops and toy shops as well as gun shops, may lead one to believe that airweapons are mere toys. The present ease with which an airweapon may be acquired is solely due to the fact that, with the exception of $CO_2$ operated weapons, the possession of a Firearm Certificate is not necessary before an air rifle or pistol may be bought. This desirable situation is under constant attack by those who are opposed to the ready availability of any sort of gun, and, although there is no evidence that with the introduction of firearms control armed crime has decreased there is not a great deal that the individual can do to combat the anti-airgun brigade, except to remember that every report of an airgun being used irresponsibly is excellent publicity for those opposed to airweapons. Safe operation must be the main consideration of all marksmen, if only because the consequences of one small ill-considered action can be lifelong.

### Safety Rules
1   Never point a gun at anyone.
2   Never shoot where you cannot see.
3   Never carry a gun uncased in a public place.
4   Never load a rifle or pistol unless it is pointing at or near a target.

In addition to the above, there are a number of rules that apply to organised shooting on ranges, where the greater number of people present increases the risk of accidents:

1  The action of a rifle or pistol is kept uncocked and un-loaded at all times when it is not actually in use.
2  The weapon is only loaded on the range, and when ready to fire is kept pointing down the range.
3  In the event of a malfunction during firing the weapon is kept pointing down the range while the fault is rectified, or assistance called for.

All the foregoing are self-explanatory, and it is worth remembering that no matter how skilled a marksman you may be, if you are not safe, no one will allow you to shoot with them.

**First Steps**

Most probably one's first acquaintance with an airweapon comes when young – shooting at tin cans in the garden supervised by father. This was certainly my introduction to guns, and when I tired of this aimless activity I turned to 'hunting' for more interest. Perhaps hunting is not the right term for shooting rabbits on a local farm, but a friend and I liked to think of it as an heroic activity. In time, our 'hunting' became more of a walk carrying guns than real shooting, and we both moved towards static target shooting as a major hobby; a transition common to many young air riflemen lacking the convenience of a nearby farm.

**Joining a Rifle Club**

While it is quite possible to enjoy target shooting with an airweapon in the confines of one's own home, the keen shooter will soon find that advice and competitions are needed if his shooting skill is to improve. A club will provide as much or as little of both as an individual may ask for, with the added bonus of a new set of friends. On the whole marksmen are convivial people, if only because they share the knowledge that the opponent is not the shooter at the next firing point, but lies within the marksman himself. Target shooting is something of a philosophical journey, the shooter pitting himself against himself, and only he knows if the game has been well played.

There is a surprisingly large number of rifle clubs in Britain, so any aspiring marksman should have no difficulty finding one near to his home. Most rifle clubs have .22 cartridge shooting as their main discipline but many have added an airweapons' section as interest in the new sport has developed. Some clubs have been founded purely to shoot airweapons, but all will be known either to the national associations, the local library or the local gun shop. By far the best way to start at a club is to be introduced by an existing member, but failing such a convenient friend, obtain the address of a local club from one of the sources mentioned above and go along one evening.

Most clubs have a fairly stringent entry requirement, usually involving a probationary period. This is not a mechanism to keep people out of the club; it is a precaution that allows the committee and the members to assess whether the applicant is a sensible person who will not be a danger to himself and others. Rifle clubs have an almost immaculate safety record, and this is brought about by strict adherence to the rules, which, in the interests of the sport, no club member will willingly see broken.

A rifle club is run on much the same lines as any club. A number of officers, usually a Chairman, Secretary, Treasurer, and Captain are supported by committee members. All these posts are held by fully paid-up members of the club, who have been elected into the executive positions by ordinary club members meeting at the Annual General Meeting. The officers and committee are responsible for the day-to-day running of the club, and generally try to ensure that the club is operated in a manner beneficial to the members. In most clubs officers and committee put themselves up for re-election every year, which gives the ordinary members a chance to change the executive, if they feel that a change would be beneficial.

Having been accepted as a probationary member, and assuming no prior knowledge of target shooting, the new member will receive some coaching from the more experienced members of the club. He may be lucky enough to have joined a club which has a beginner's coaching scheme, but in any event the beginner must not be afraid to ask for help. Most shooters are only too happy to help, but are diffident about volunteering advice where it is not requested. As one progresses with target shooting, so one becomes aware of all the variable factors that must be controlled if consistently good scores are to be achieved. The rate of progress naturally depends on the individual, but provided one has the strength to hold the weapon, and good enough eyesight (with or without glasses) to see the sights and the target, there is no reason why young or old, male or female, the novice should not become a fine marksman.

Generally, club premises are fairly sparse, but where possible, are divided into three sections: the range itself, a gun room where weapons are prepared, and a club room for members to relax in. It is the usual convention that guns are not taken into the club room unless cased, and while this restriction is often relaxed these days a new member is well advised to be aware that such local rules may exist and can prove a pitfall. It is also worth mentioning that one never handles a gun that belongs to someone else without first being given specific permission.

All clubs provide rifles and pistols for the use of members, and for the novice airgunner, who may only possess one of the cheaper recoiling weapons, this is an excellent and inexpensive way to try out a variety of the more sophisticated guns. While it is quite possible to spend one's shooting career using club weapons, the serious shooter will soon want to buy his own weapons, if only to be assured that the sights have not been altered from one day to the next. When buying a gun it always pays to buy the best you can afford − even if you can't really afford it.

Soon, sooner than a beginner may expect, he will find the

captain asking if he would like to shoot in a team. Most clubs will field as many teams as there are members willing to shoot, and since competing teams are matched on the basis of their aggregate averages there is every chance of fair competition at whatever level matches are made.

## Competitions

Shooting competitions fall into two categories: shoulder-to-shoulder, or postal. Shoulder-to-shoulder competitions are those matches that take place on one range, with all the competitors shooting 'shoulder-to-shoulder' in a series of groups known as 'details' or 'squads'. All the major competitions are shoulder-to-shoulder; the National Championships, International and Olympic matches all being fired by competitors present on the designated range. Shoulder-to-shoulder shoots have two notable features: they provide match experience for competitors, and the chance to meet shooters from other parts of the country and even other parts of the world. A shoulder-to-shoulder 'Open' meeting is a chance to watch and talk to world champions, a chance to try to emulate them, and, at the very least, excellent experience for any novice shooter.

Of course, such a meeting is expensive and complex to organise, and so 'postal' shooting has become the mainstay of club shooting in the United Kingdom. As the name suggests, targets are shot either by individuals or teams, duly signed and witnessed, and then posted to a collection point where they are scored and the results notified to the competitors. By this manner, shooters throughout Britain can compete against each other summer and winter, without ever meeting. And that, in many ways, is the only disadvantage of postal matches.

## Some Common Shooting Terms

A target, you might think, is a target. Not so, or rather, not necessarily so. To a marksman that piece of paper at which he shoots is called a 'card'. The concentric circles printed

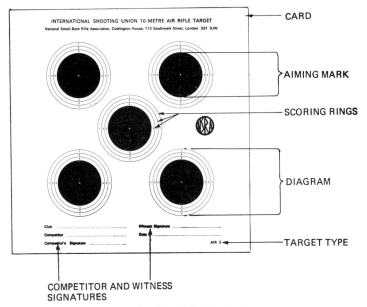

**3** 10m five bull rifle target

thereon are the 'scoring rings', the solid black circle in the centre is the 'aiming mark', and the 'bull' is just as often referred to as the 'ten', from, of course, the number of points scored when it is hit. The combination of the scoring rings and aiming mark is referred to as a 'diagram', an important point when one considers that a 10m air rifle 'card' consists of 5 'diagrams', all of which have to be fired at individually (Fig 3). All this may seem needlessly complex − why not fire away at one target, and after ten shots stop and count up? The explanation lies in the incredible accuracy of modern target weapons. An expert shot is able to put ten shots practically on top of each other, so clearly it would be impossible to score such a card as it would consist solely of one hole. And so targets evolved with a number of diagrams, the marksman being required to fire one shot, or sometimes two shots, on each, making a total of five or ten scoring shots per card.

The great accuracy of modern weapons has also affected

4 Good grouping, but a low score

the manner in which scores are reckoned. It is tedious to keep adding up nines, eights, tens and so on, so a marksman adds up the points *lost* and deducts the total from the possible total for a card. So 97 out of 100 becomes 'three off', 99 is 'one off' and 100 out of 100 is called a 'poss' or 'possible' (from highest possible score).

Much shooting talk centres around 'groups' and 'grouping'. These terms rule a shooter's life, and refer simply to how a string of shots form around their mean point of impact (mpi). Without becoming involved in theory, suffice it to say that to a marksman, the actual place in which shots fall on a card is not as important as their dispersion. A small 'group' off to the left (Fig 4) can be moved to the centre of

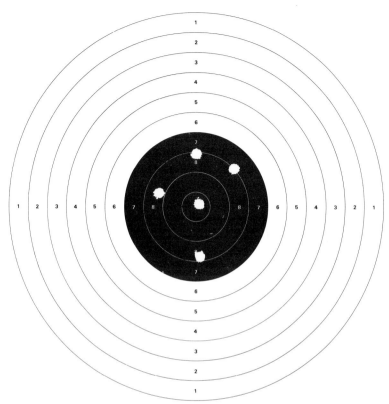

5 Bad grouping, but a higher score than that in Fig 4

the card by a simple sight adjustment, and is thus potentially better shooting than a group made up of shots scattered all over the card (Fig 5). The latter may initially score higher, but the tight group will, after suitable alignment of sights, provide a better long-term result.

The value of a shot on a target is taken from the scoring ring in which the shot falls. Because the pellet does not cut a perfectly clean hole exactly to its own dimensions, it is often impossible to say from unaided eye judgement whether a shot has just touched, or just missed a particular scoring ring. To help scorers in this matter, a small metal plug, called a 'gauge', is employed. The gauge, which is machined to an exact size, is placed delicately into the doubtful shot hole and its outer edges are examined through a magnifying glass to verify the score. Insertion gauges may only be used on competition cards by official scorers, their use by anyone else renders the card void, as they slightly enlarge the shot hole and thus could be used for cheating. There is, however, a type of gauge available which can be used legally on a competition card by the competitor keen to know his exact score. This device is a small transparent plastic tube with a magnifying lens at one end and engraved rings at the other, the careful placement of which over the doubtful shot hole will indicate the value scored.

Any keen shooter spends a great deal of time shooting competition, or 'match' cards; the chief difference between practice cards and match cards is that the latter must be properly signed and witnessed. This procedure is laid down by the national and international governing bodies, but is briefly as follows. Before shooting a match card the shooter's name must be on the card, complete with any stickers required by the conditions of the particular competition. After shooting, the shooter must sign the card and pass it to an official witness, who must also sign and date the card. The official witness can either be a senior member of one of the governing bodies, or, as is more usual, one or another of the members of a club who have been nominated by their club as official witnesses.

# 2 Airweapons

## The Parts of an Airweapon

In order to discuss various aspects of airweapon design, it is clearly important to have a commonly understood designation for the various parts of a rifle or pistol. Naturally, all rifles and pistols have certain features in common, and airweapons are no exception, but they do have some additional features, peculiar to their compressed air functions. In fact, strange as it may seem, a fine airweapon is a more complex piece of engineering than an equivalent firearm, and this accounts for the high cost of many airweapons.

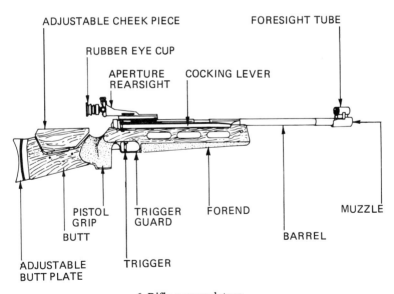

6 Rifle nomenclature

## The Air Rifle

Considering the rifle from the 'sharp end', the foresight, muzzle and barrel are well known and self-explanatory. The 'stock' is a common word and strictly refers to all the woodwork which supports the barrel and enables the weapon to be held by the shooter. More precisely, the stock can be considered as two main parts, and on some rifles the stock is actually fashioned from two separate pieces of wood (a 'two-piece' stock) as opposed to the more usual 'one-piece' stock. Under the barrel, one encounters the 'fore-end' − that piece of the stock designed to be supported by the shooter's non-trigger hand. The fore-end can be a variety of shapes, usually determined by the use to which the rifle is to be put. Generally speaking, rifles for shooting at static targets (Fig 7) have broad, deep fore-ends to enable a marksman to balance them firmly on his hand. Rifles for hunting or shooting at moving targets (Fig 8) have slimmer, tapered fore-ends to enable them to be gripped easily as the weapon is being swung during the aim.

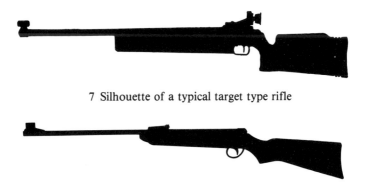

7 Silhouette of a typical target type rifle

8 Silhouette of a typical sporting type rifle

The second part of the stock − the butt, also differs in shape with its function, tending to be slimmer and more raked on hunting rifles than on target weapons. Modern developments have revolutionised the design of the butt, from being merely that piece of the stock placed in the shoulder, to a complex ergonomic device which must be correctly adjusted to ensure consistently good results. On a modern air rifle, the butt plate is usually adjustable for height (Fig 9) to enable the sight line to be raised and lowered; the face of the butt is equipped with a 'cheek-piece' to give a comfortable support to the shooter's face, and the small of the butt is designed to give a comfortable hold for the trigger hand, usually in the form of a pistol grip, or occasionally, for moving-target competitions, with a thumb hole through the stock.

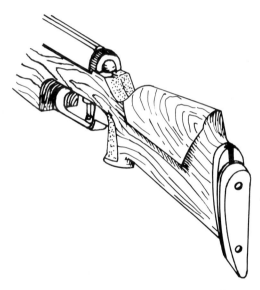

9 Rifle butt showing contoured cheek-piece

Lying alongside, or sometimes underneath the barrel, is the cocking lever, the operation of which cocks the rifle and usually opens the breech to allow pellets to be inserted into the loading tap. The barrel may be equipped with blocks for the attachment of telescopic sights, but in any event there will be some form of back sight. This can vary from a simple assembly to a sophisticated micrometer screw arrangement.

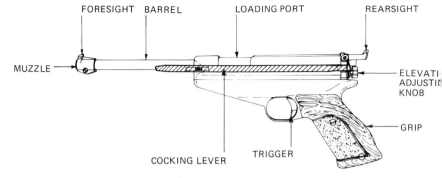

FORESIGHT  BARREL  LOADING PORT  REARSIGHT

MUZZLE

ELEVATI
ADJUSTIN
KNOB

GRIP

COCKING LEVER  TRIGGER

10 Pistol nomenclature

### The Air Pistol

In many respects an air pistol differs little from a rifle. Obviously it is much smaller, being designed to be fired from one hand, and much lighter, but its major functions are basically the same as those of the rifle. The cocking action is similar, being either break-barrel or cocking lever, and the design of the trigger mechanism, though requiring to be set to a heavier pull than that of the rifle, follows the general pattern of a rifle action. Perhaps the most important differences between the rifle and pistol are in the sights and grip. Pistol sights are always 'open sights', and never the aperture sights favoured on rifles, since the latter would be impossibly difficult to use because of the great distance between the sighting eye and the rear sight of a pistol.

For the pistoleer it is of vital importance that the pistol can be gripped in an identical manner from shot to shot. In essence this means fitting a pistol with a stock designed expressly for the hand of the individual who will fire the pistol. Such a grip is known as 'anatomical', and some of the better pistols are sold with such a grip as an option. Even so it is unlikely that any mass-produced grip will fit every hand which fires the pistol, and so a 'custom' grip becomes necessary. These can be ordered from specialist gunsmiths, but many pistoleers fashion their own, either out of solid wood blocks or, more easily, by building on an existing grip

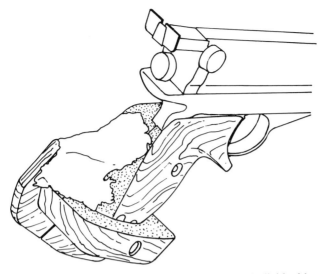

11 Pistol grip modified with plastic wood to suit an individual hand

with plastic wood (Fig 11). Clearly such operations cannot be carried out on a club weapon, and so it is of paramount importance that any person intent on serious pistol shooting must own his own weapon.

## Recoil

The problem of recoil is particularly acute in an airweapon as opposed to a firearm, because the pellet spends much longer in the barrel of an airweapon. This is because of the time taken for the spring to build up pressure before the pellet begins to move, and the subsequently slow progress of the pellet down the barrel. In the case of a firearm, most recoil takes place after the bullet has left the weapon, so having less effect on accuracy. The contrary is true of an airweapon, and much ingenuity has been used to design 'recoilless' air rifles and pistols. This has been achieved in three main ways:

1  Using stored gas under pressure, $CO_2$ or air.
2  Using two pistons working against each other to cancel out the recoil.
3  Arranging for the body of the weapon to slide back at the

moment of firing, thus preventing the transmission of recoil effects.

Some authorities maintain that recoilless weapons are not necessary for the attainment of great accuracy, and certainly this is true of airweapons used for hunting, but in national and international championships no major award has ever been won by an airweapon without a recoilless action. Most of the recoilless weapons currently available are made in Europe, and although expensive, are essential for competition shooting.

**Cocking Actions**
Whatever form of propulsion is used, all airweapons must be cocked and loaded. With the exception of $CO_2$ powered weapons, this action involves either compressing a fairly

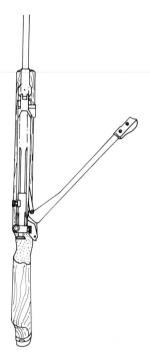

12  Side lever cocking

13 Break-barrel cocking

powerful spring or a quantity of air in a chamber. There are two basic systems for achieving this − the break-barrel or the cocking lever (Figs 12 and 13).

The former is the older system and consists simply of the shooter unlocking the barrel and drawing it downwards against the spring pressure. When compression is complete the spring is locked by the trigger mechanism, the shooter places a pellet in the exposed loading tap and then closes the weapon, which is ready to fire. The advantage of this system lies in the ease with which a strong spring can be compressed, the leverage given by a long barrel being considerable. Because of this facility, break-barrel actions are often found on high-powered hunting weapons, but for the target marksman the system has two main disadvantages. Firstly, breaking the barrel to load can be a considerable inconvenience on a crowded firing line, but more importantly the disturbance caused to the sight line by the continuous movement of the barrel is a variable factor best avoided.

It is an oddity of airweapons that accuracy is not dependent on high power; quite the reverse, in fact, the more important consideration being consistency from shot to shot. Clearly a weapon in which the barrel, and with it the sight, is moved from shot to shot is unlikely to reach the standards of consistency required by a competition marksman, so an alternative system is needed. The answer lies in the provision of a cocking lever. This lever is usually placed alongside or underneath a fixed barrel and its operation compresses the spring, or charges the cylinder with air. In some weapons it also opens the loading tap to enable the shooter to insert a pellet into the barrel.

## Care and Cleaning

Like most precision equipment, air rifles and pistols will function for many years, provided they are handled as the manufacturer intended. It is surprisingly easy to do permanent damage to a weapon. Obviously dropping a rifle or pistol is going to have a serious effect, but less obvious mishandling can be as damaging. Never fire a weapon if there is a chance that any grit or other dirt has found its way into the barrel or action. Small particles can ease their way into a weapon if it has been rested on the ground, or even left open outside on a windy day, and such particles can have a disastrous effect on the functioning of a weapon.

When carrying a rifle it should be supported evenly at the point of balance under the fore-end − holding a rifle by the barrel while carrying the body of the weapon over the shoulder may look very well in a cowboy film, but it can damage the bedding or the barrel. For transport to and from the shooting range, a carrying case should be used, both for rifles and pistols. Carrying cases range from strong boxes with foam rubber inserts to floppy canvas cases. Obviously the stronger box is the better, but any form of gun cover is preferable to slinging the weapon unprotected into the boot of a car. When a rifle is not cased and not in use, it should be stood upright on its butt and lightly supported at the top of the barrel. The traditional vertical gun rack is an excellent method of storing rifles before or between shoots. There is no really satisfactory form of rack for pistols, and so the preferred method with an air pistol is to leave it cased until actually shooting, and then to return it to its case immediately after firing. Air rifles and pistols must always be handled with delicacy − in many instances an airweapon is a finer piece of machinery than a watch, and often costs much more.

Cleaning is a much debated subject. For every shooter who believes in careful cleaning of weapons, there are at least two who are sure that all is best left well alone. Clearly as both total neglect and permanent tampering are undesirable, a sensible balance must be struck. It is probably fair to say that the amount of cleaning necessary will depend on usage. Since lead pellets and the propellant air are clean, no burnt powder compounds remain to corrode the barrel. Corrosion can be caused by damp storage of a weapon, but this problem is unlikely to effect a keen shooter who fires his weapon at least once a week. To a certain extent the infrequent shooter will probably need to do more cleaning than an active marksman, so the following suggestions are intended as a basis which may be modified according to the needs of the individual shooter.

After shooting, a light wipe over the metal areas with an oily rag will keep the weapon free of corrosion. As a general rule the stock is best left untreated. Some shooters use furniture polish on wooden stocks, but any treatment which makes the stock slippery is not to be recommended. Sights should be kept clean and free of grease, and they may benefit from being 'blacked' either in the smoke of a candle, or by being treated with one of the proprietary blacking compounds.

For the average shooter, stripping a weapon is fraught with peril. For the airgun shooter, it can also be dangerous as all spring-operated guns are under considerable tension, even when uncocked, so complete disassembly is best left to experts. Such major work should only be necessary at long intervals. Far more important to the airweapon is the periodic lubrication of the accessible moving parts. Most airweapons are supplied with a note of the makers recommended lubrication schedule and this should be followed with the possible addition of an occasional oiling through the barrel. This can be achieved either by using an oiled felt patch on a cleaning rod or 'pull through', or by shooting some felt pellets through the weapon. In any event, a 'non-dieseling' oil should be used, as ordinary oils will be ignited in the barrel by the heat generated during firing. This affects the accuracy of the shot, and if repeated often enough will result in permanent damage to the barrel. As a further precaution, it is wise to dry any excess oil from inside the barrel immediately prior to shooting, by passing a clean felt patch or felt pellet through the weapon several times, or until no further oil marks are left on the cloth.

**Weapons Reviewed**

Today there is a bewildering variety of air rifles and pistols available, ranging in price from a few pounds to several hundred. While it is generally true that one gets what one pays for, it is not necessarily true that the most expensive airweapon is the one to go out and buy, as a cheap weapon may well suit a particular person's needs better than an expensive Continental model. To make consideration of the many weapons available easier, I am adopting a classification of my own, and dividing airweapons into two categories – leisure or target. This is really only a convenience because the categories do overlap, but as a generality the two terms nicely separate the two distinct types of airweapon.

**Leisure**

Into this category are placed airweapons which are used for hunting, vermin control, shooting at tin cans in the garden and those informal competitions which come under the title of 'plinking'. Weapons for leisure shooting are generally of .22 calibre as this size, coupled with a high muzzle velocity, produces most satisfactory effects on the target when hit. Recoilless actions are seldom necessary for leisure airweapons, and this factor means that such pistols and rifles are usually in the cheap or medium price range. Leisure weapons are usually supplied fitted with rudimentary open sights and mounting blocks for telescopic sights, the latter usually purchased as an accessory. It is quite impossible to consider in detail all the airweapons currently available, and so I have chosen to review a number of popular models. The comments are based on my own observations coupled with opinions expressed by other shooters whose views I respect. It is as well to remember that opinions are only opinions, not statements of irrefutable fact.

LEISURE RIFLES
*BSA Meteor*

Calibre: .177 and .22.   Length: 42in.   Weight: 6lb

The Meteor has been the mainstay of the BSA air rifle range for many years. Indeed, my first air rifle, some twenty years ago, was a Meteor, and a great deal of fun it provided. The Meteor was then, as it is now, a good basic air rifle. Enough power and accuracy for vermin shooting, light enough to carry around, and a reasonable if crude trigger. The action is cocked by breaking the barrel, and the pellet inserted directly into the breech. The rifle is equipped with adjustable open sights, but is also dovetailed for telescopic sights which can be bought as an extra. The Meteor is sold complete with target holder, targets, some pellets, gun oil and full instructions, and is an excellent beginner's air rifle, although anyone becoming very interested in air rifle shooting would need to buy a more sophisticated rifle to fully enjoy the hobby. A Super Meteor is available with the same barrel and action fitted in a different stock, furnished with a cheek piece and recoil pad.

*BSA Mercury*

Calibre: .177 and .22.   Length: 43in.   Weight: 7lb

This air rifle falls in the middle of the BSA range, being somewhat more powerful than the Meteor and having a more raked and 'sporty' stock. The cocking action is of break-barrel type, and the rifle is available in two versions: standard, with a plain stock, and super, with a chequered stock. The Mercury is an excellent air rifle for vermin shooting and is one of the most popular British air rifles.

## BSA Airsporter-S

Calibre: .177 and .22.   Length: 45in.   Weight: 8lb

The Airsporter-S is the top of the BSA range and employs similar internal mechanism to the Mercury, but features underlever cocking and loading through a tap. The Airsporter-S is a very handsome rifle, owing its looks to the chequered shotgun-like stock, cheek-piece and ventilated recoil pad. The trigger is adjustable, and although the rifle is equipped with adjustable open sights, the receiver is dovetailed for the attachment of telescopic sights, available as an extra. A powerful, reasonably accurate air rifle that should last a hunter many years of small game shooting.

## Webley Vulcan

Calibre: .177 and .22.   Length: 41in.   Weight: 7lb

The Vulcan is the most powerful air rifle in the Webley range and is intended primarily for small game shooting. The stock is of Beech and fairly utilitarian in appearance. The cocking action is break-barrel and the cylinder is dovetailed for telescopic sights. The rifle is rugged and gives the impression of being a workaday, no frills weapon, well suited to use on a farm.

## Webley Osprey and Supertarget

Osprey—Calibre: .177 and .22.   Length: 43in.   Weight: 8lb
Supertarget—Calibre: .177.   Length: 44in.   Weight: 8½lb

The Osprey is a side lever cocking rifle intended primarily for fun shooting. It is somewhat low on power for effective vermin shooting, and rather noisy to cock. The stock is plain, with a hunting pattern butt and square fore-end. The rifle is fairly accurate, which possibly persuaded Webley to introduce the Osprey Supertarget version. This target rifle has a competition stock, heavy barrel and a micrometer aperture rearsight. Sadly, the weapon is not recoilless, has a rather heavy trigger and retails for a price very near to that of a Continental recoilless rifle. No British manufacturer has yet produced a real competition air rifle, but we live in hope.

## Original 45/45S

Calibre: .177 and .22.   Length: 45in.   Weight: 8lb

A very powerful, accurate hunting air rifle from West Germany. The cocking action is break-barrel, and features an automatic safety catch, placed at the end of the cylinder within easy reach of the right hand. This rifle is heavy and very noisy on firing, but is solid, well made, and is proving popular in Britain. The 45S is a *de luxe* version sold complete with sling and barrel weight but without sights, allowing the shooter to fit his own telescopic sight.

## Weihrauch HW35

Calibre: .177 and .22.   Length: 45in.   Weight: 8½lb

This rifle is a popular hunting weapon from West Germany. Its rather heavy weight is compensated for by high power and reasonable accuracy. It is very noisy in operation and the trigger is rather stiff. A target rearsight is available for the HW35 but it is not suitable as a target weapon, if only because the noise of its firing would disturb other shooters. The HW35 has a well finished stock, rubber recoil pad, and is supplied complete with four foresight elements. An excellent, economical buy for the small game shooter.

LEISURE PISTOLS
## Walther LP53

Calibre: .177 and .22.   Length: 11in.   Weight: 2½lb

Although considered by some commentators to be a target pistol, the LP53 is really only suitable as a leisure weapon, or for use in training for cartridge pistols. The LP53 has a familiar silhouette, being the weapon used in the publicity photographs for the early James Bond films. It features break-barrel cocking, which can be quite difficult as the weapon has a short barrel and strong spring, and a fully adjustable, if crude, rear sight. The grips are plastic and quite chunky. The pistol has a fair amount of vibration on firing, but has a good trigger and is generally pleasant to handle. It is not cheap, but is very well made, and should last a lifetime of not too serious shooting.

*Webley Hurricane*

Calibre: .177 and .22.   Length: 11in.   Weight: 2½lb

The current range of Webley pistols comprises three weapons: Tempest, an unsophisticated junior pistol; the Typhoon, a more powerful weapon but with small grips for youngsters; and the Hurricane, with full-size grips and a strong mainspring. All three pistols use the unique time-honoured Webley cocking system; the barrel breaks at the breech and is rotated through 100 degrees forwards over the cylinder to cock the action and is returned prior to firing. On firing, the piston travels towards the rear of the pistol and the venting air is turned through 180 degrees and directed into the barrel behind the pellet. The design feature of having the barrel lying over the cylinder enables Webley pistols to be powerful without being over-long, and they do balance quite comfortably in the hand. The Hurricane is a good general purpose pistol, although its trigger leaves a great deal to be desired. The pistol can also be fitted with a telescopic sight, and is sold packaged in a stout cardboard box which doubles as a storage case for the pistol, 'scope sight, target holder and pellets.

## Original 66

Calibre: .177.   Length: 16in.   Weight: 3lb

The Original model 6 series were the first spring recoilless air pistols in the world, and the 66 is an excellent pistol at a reasonable price. It incorporates competition style grips, and would be a useful competition weapon but for the foresight with which it is equipped; a type not allowed under international rules. A good general purpose pistol for someone requiring accuracy rather than power.

## Crosman 1377 and 1322

Calibre: .177 (1377) and .22 (1322).   Length: 14in.   Weight: 2½lb

These pistols are pump up pneumatics, with a sliding breech cover through which the pellet is inserted. The cylinder is charged with air by pumping the fore-end, which is the cocking lever, any number of times between two and ten, which gives maximum power. The weapon is made ready for firing by pulling out a knurled knob at the end of the cylinder. In action the pistol that I tried was quite unpleasant, being badly balanced, having very thin grips and an inadequate sighting system. The trigger let-off was surprisingly bad for a pneumatic pistol, and my feeling was that only an extension shoulder stock would render this pistol suitable for any serious use.

## BSA Scorpion

Calibre: .177 and .22.   Length: 16in.   Weight: 3¼lb

The Scorpion is the only air pistol made by BSA and is a fairly meaty, man-size weapon. It is cocked and loaded by breaking the barrel, an operation made easier by a removable cocking piece which attaches to the muzzle and looks not unlike a muzzle brake. This extension piece can be left in place while firing, and it certainly makes depressing the powerful spring easier. The Scorpion has a plastic, chequered grip of sizeable proportions, and the balance of the pistol would, I think, suit anyone with fairly large hands. A pistol 'scope is available as an extra, and with it in place the pistol would be excellent for close range vermin shooting although its fairly heavy kick may take some getting used to.

**Target**
The design of airweapons for competitive shooting is highly specialised: they must, under international rules, be of .177 (4.5mm) calibre only; pistols are restricted as to weight, dimensions and trigger pull. Rifles are restricted as to weight and certain accessories. And of course, target airweapons must be accurate: a 'one hole' group of ten shots at 10m is an average standard for both pistols and rifles. Most target airweapons currently available are of recoilless design and Continental manufacture. The Germans pioneered and still lead the field of target airguns, their dominance being a result of restrictions placed on their firearms industry by the victors of World War II. Competition airweapons are either expensive or very expensive, but often second-hand target guns are an excellent purchase.

TARGET AIR RIFLES
*Walther LGR, LGR Match and Universal*

Calibre: .177. Length: 45.5in. Barrel: 19.5in. Weight: 11lb. Muzzle velocity: 560fps. Right- and left-hand versions available

This series of air rifles uses pneumatic propulsion − the outward stroke of the cocking lever collects air in the cylinder, which is compressed by the inward stroke. The pellet is inserted into the barrel via a separately operated loading tap which is closed manually before firing. The trigger mechanism acts on the valve retaining the compressed air, allowing the air to expand rapidly and thus drive the pellet down the barrel. This complete absence of large moving parts makes the Walther a totally vibrationless weapon; indeed there is hardly any movement at the moment of firing, the shooter being aware only of a slight interruption in the process of holding the weapon steady. The only difficulty, which can be overcome with practise, is that the return stroke of the cocking lever requires a fair amount of effort as the air is compressed.

The LGR is the standard air rifle, and a version, the LGR Match, is available with a raised sight line and raised cheek piece for those shooters who prefer the head-up position; the Universal has an adjustable stock. All rifles are sold complete with aperture sights, spare foresight elements, cleaning kit, and a few other bits and pieces. The workmanship of these Walther rifles is in a class of its own, their accuracy is phenomenal and they can fairly be considered among the best three air rifle makes in the world. My own personal favourite.

*Feinwerkbau 300S/SU*

Calibre: .177. Length: 43in. Barrel 20in. Weight: 10.75lb. Muzzle velocity: 580fps. Right- and left-hand versions available

For many years the top international prizes have been taken by marksmen using Feinwerkbau weapons and no other manufacturer has yet had such success. Unlike the Walther, Feinwerkbau rifles do use a moving piston to discharge the pellet, recoilless operation being achieved by allowing the entire barrel and action assembly to slide back on the stock at the moment of firing. Thus there is some mechanical movement, but as it takes place after the pellet has left the weapon it cannot affect accuracy. The 300S rifle differs from the SU only in that the latter has an interchangeable cheek piece for shooting in the head-up position, raised sights and a differently shaped fore-end. Both rifles are sold complete with sights, foresight elements and two basic tools; with the SU are supplied a spare comb and a butt spacer. The trigger is fully adjustable for position and weight, and the action is one of the finest on any air rifle. The Feinwerkbau 300S and SU are quite capable of taking a shooter to World Championship class, and can be expected to function satisfactorily for a lifetime.

### Original 66 and 75

Calibre: .177. Length: 44in. Barrel length: 18in. Weight: Model 66, 11lb, reduced to 9lb on removal of barrel sleeve; Model 75: 11lb. Right- and left-handed versions available

Both these rifles are recoilless, using the principle of opposing pistons, the 66 being a cheaper weapon well suited to the novice. Both rifles use the same action, but the 66 is cocked by breaking the barrel whereas the 75 has side lever cocking. In operation both rifles are recoilless, but I find the metallic noise transmitted through the stock rather disconcerting. The 75 is also available in a high-stocked version, designated the 75HV, and either of the 75 models are capable of very high match performances. All models are sold complete with aperture sights, foresight elements and composite screwdriver. My only criticism of these otherwise excellent rifles is that they do not seem to have the fine finish of the Walther and Feinwerkbau rifles.

### Anschutz 250

Calibre: .177. Length: 45in. Weight: 10¾lb

This target air rifle features side lever cocking and a form of recoilless action but is not currently in favour with top level marksmen. Despite this, the Anschutz is capable of considerable accuracy and, as its sights are interchangeable with those of the .22 cartridge match rifles, the 250 could be useful as a training weapon. The 250 is best considered as a beginner's target weapon, and it will be superceded when the new Anschutz recoilless air rifle comes into production.

## Walther LGV Special and Junior

Calibre: .177.   Length: 42in.   Weight: 11lb

These two rifles use the same barrel and action, but the Junior is lighter and shorter than the Special. Both rifles are well made and capable of high levels of accuracy, but are not of recoilless design. This factor, coupled with the rather high purchase price, tends to make them an unattractive proposition when, for a little more money, a rifleman can buy a true recoilless weapon. Nevertheless both weapons are made to the usual high standards of Walther, and were the top of that company's range until the advent of the recoilless LGR series. Break-barrel cocking.

TARGET PISTOLS

## Feinwerkbau 65 and 85

Calibre: .177.   Sight base: 14½in.   Weight: Under 3lb

The Feinwerkbau 65 pistol has been the most successful target air pistol ever made. To date the type has held every title and record open to it, and is only gradually being superceded by the model 85. Both pistols use the same action, but the 85 has a modified trigger and a facility for adding weight under the barrel to change the centre of gravity. Both the pistols are recoilless, using the Feinwerkbau sliding action principle, and feature side-lever cocking. Both pistols are available with a number of grip options: plastic, walnut and anatomical, the latter being an adjustable, shaped, wooden grip much favoured by the top marksmen. For left-handers there is an appropriate anatomical grip, and all pistols are supplied with adjustable sights, an additional foresight blade and a combination spanner. Compared with other target pistols, the FWB sits very low in the hand, which gives extra stability with the dropped wrist firing position, and superb balance. Anyone interested in air pistol competition should consider the Feinwerkbau pistols very seriously; at the time of writing they can fairly be considered to be the best in the world.

*FAS AP 604*

Calibre: .177.   Sight base: 9in.   Weight: under 2½lb
without weights

This Italian pistol is very much a newcomer to British airweapon shooting, but is already a very popular weapon, being
of excellent quality and reasonable price. The gun is based on
the very successful FAS series of .22 cartridge rapid fire pistols
and shares with them a similarity of design, trigger action and
stock. The air pistol uses pneumatic propulsion, the cylinder
being charged and the trigger cocked by rotating the top rib
and barrel forward through 100 degrees, an action not unlike
that of Webley's series of air pistols. The pellet is inserted into
the barrel during the cocking procedure, and the weapon
prepared for action by snapping the top rib back into place.

In action the pistol that I tried was superb. The grip,
straight from the box, was an excellent fit; the pistol was
supplied with a medium grip, but eight options are available
– three sizes in both left- and right-handed form and two
ladies' grips – and the trigger was one of the best I have tried.
It is adjustable in four functions: 1st stage, 2nd stage, weight
and travel. With the adjustable stop, it is probably the most
comprehensive trigger mechanism fitted to any air pistol. The
let-off is clean and definite, like the breaking of a thin glass
rod. At under 2½lb the pistol is quite light and some feeling
of gas reaction is apparent on firing. I did not find this
excessive, but the addition of one of the two barrel weights
supplied should help to dampen this effect.

The pistol is engineered and finished to a high standard,
and is sold complete with adjustable sights, barrel weights, a
spare 'O' ring and some tools. To my mind this is the
championship weapon of the very near future.

*Walther LP3 and LP3 Match*

Calibre: .177.   Sight base: 13in.   Weight: Under 3lb

The LP3 pistol is the only recoilless air pistol in the Walther range, and it uses the pneumatic system favoured by Walther for their air rifles. The cocking lever forms part of the trigger guard and grip and is operated in two strokes: the outward collects air in a cylinder in the pistol butt, the return compresses and holds the air ready for firing. This return stroke takes very considerable effort and could be a handicap in a long course of fire, although with practise it becomes easier. The pistol is loaded by breaking the barrel and inserting the pellet in the exposed breech. In action the pistol has no mechanical movement, the shooter receiving only a small sensation of reaction from the air expanding. The trigger let-off is superb, and it is surprising that the Walther pistols have not enjoyed more success in international competition. The LP3 Match is essentially the same as the LP3, with the exception of the grip, which on the Match pistol is of adjustable anatomical type while the LP3 is equipped with only the standard plastic grip. Both pistols are expensive, but are being seen in increasing numbers on firing points.

## Original 6M

Calibre: .177.   Sight base: 14in.   Weight: 3lb

This pistol is of recoilless design, using the opposing pistons system favoured by Original. Cocking and loading is effected by breaking the barrel, an operation made easier by a unique Original feature: the barrel is contained within an outer sleeve which is rotated manually through 180 degrees to both protect the foresight, and provide a better lever for the hand to grip. This clever device makes cocking the pistol an easy operation, despite the rather short barrel. The grip of the pistol is plastic, comfortable but rather thin and so does not settle easily into a repeatable position in the hand. The trigger has a limited amount of adjustment available and is rounded in section, which I find not as satisfactory as a square section. Nevertheless, the let-off is quite smooth. I find that the pistol is somewhat muzzle heavy and because of this is not as naturally stable as the Feinwerkbau 65. This is a purely personal observation, but the 'feel' of a pistol is a very important consideration and one that can dramatically influence a marksman's performance. For those who are happy with its balance, Original 6M is an excellent and not very expensive target pistol.

## Original 10

Calibre: .177.   Sight base: Adjustable.   Weight: 3lb

This pistol is similar in many ways to the 6M, being recoilless and employing the same cocking system. Additionally the model 10 has a fully adjustable trigger and an adjustable walnut anatomic stock. This pistol is available boxed in a presentation case complete with screwdrivers, pellets, targets and instruction book, or in a cheaper version which has plastic grips and is packed in a modest cardboard box.

## Daisy 717

Calibre: .177.   Sight base: 13in.   Weight: Under 3lb

This pistol is a newcomer to Britain and consequently not a great deal is known of its potential. It has, however, two features which make it a good pistol for the beginner. It is of pneumatic recoilless type and retails at about half the cost of the cheapest recoilless target pistol otherwise available. The Daisy features a side-cocking lever, the action of which charges the air cylinder and compresses the air ready for firing. A small manually operated bolt is used to locate the pellet in the barrel, an action not unlike that of a cartridge rifle, and closure of the bolt makes the pistol ready for firing. There is no appreciable mechanical movement of the pistol on firing, but there is quite a noticeable reaction as the compressed air expands. The trigger of the pistol is rather poor, being heavy and stiff in use. There are no adjustments available on the trigger, and this is the single biggest disadvantage of this weapon. The pistol is fitted with a safety catch, adjustable rear sight and the plastic grips are available in left-hand as well as right-hand configurations. I think it is fair to say that the Daisy is not as rugged as the more expensive target air pistols, and could not be expected to last a lifetime of high-level competition.

## Buying a Second-hand Gun

Perhaps the most important advice on this subject is the oft-repeated phrase: buy from a reputable dealer. There are, however, a few tests that purchasers can apply to help eliminate really bad buys. Firstly, consider the external appearance of the weapon: are the sights firm, the gunmetal and woodwork clean and unmarked, the barrel tight in the stock, the cocking and loading mechanisms functioning crisply and correctly? The outside appearance is usually a good guide to the interior, so if the exterior is acceptable, proceed to the interior. Check inside the barrel for rust; if in doubt, push a clean patch on a rod once through to the muzzle. Any rust will show clearly on the patch and such a gun should be rejected at once. To establish the accuracy of the weapon it will be necessary to fire a number of pellets, preferably using some form of rest. If a gunshop is not able to allow a test firing on the premises, then arrange to take the weapon away on approval. This a reasonable request − no one would buy a second-hand car without a test drive − so a refusal to allow the test firing of an airweapon must be viewed with suspicion.

The test firing, apart from establishing accuracy, will also allow a number of other important factors to be assessed: do the sights move freely and accurately, is the trigger smooth and consistent, do the fixing screws loosen after a number of shots have been fired? It is probably fair to say that target airweapons receive greater care from their owners than leisure guns, and that, coupled with their high quality of construction, often makes them worth buying second-hand.

# 3 Ammunition and Accessories

## Ammunition

There is a surprising variety of different pellets available for the airweapon shooter. Most are made purely of lead, and this is a requirement of pellets used in competitive target shooting, but there are many patterns available.

### BB

14 BB pellet

There seems to be no agreement on the derivation of the term 'BB', the most favoured explanation being that it is shorthand for 'ball bearings'. Certainly BB shot (Fig 14) could be mistaken for ball bearings, as the pellets are small spherical balls not unlike the shotgun ammunition of the same name. BB is used extensively in America where the Daisy company is the world's largest manufacturer of the type, chiefly as ammunition for plinking. BB ammunition consists of steel spheres coated with copper to prevent rust, but they are not noted for accuracy, particularly over longer ranges. They are, however, the only sort of ammunition practicable for use in air machine-guns. Such esoteric weapons are available in the United States, but are usually confined to fairground amusement stalls in the United Kingdom. It is probably fair to say that for most air gunners, the BB pellet is used very early in a career and then later discarded in favour of more accurate patterns.

### THE DIABOLO

15 Diabolo pellet

The diabolo design (Fig 15), the familiar 'waisted' pellet with the flaired skirt, is of German origin and is said to take its name from an ancient Greek juggling game. The diagram shows the standard diabolo pellet with a rounded head. The waisted design of the diabolo, coupled with the hollow base, places most of the weight of the pellet forward in the head. This aids stability in flight and thus accuracy. The head of the pellet rides lightly on the rifling of the barrel, and it is the tail of the skirt which is gripped by the lands, thus providing an air seal. From this it can be seen that the accuracy of the diabolo pellet depends largely on the skirt being undamaged, so it pays to reject any pellets that are dented.

WADCUTTER                        16 Wadcutter pellet

While the basic design of the diabolo pellet is well proven, there are a number of specialised variations. The target marksman requires a pellet that will cut a clean hole in the card, and so the aptly named 'wadcutter', a diabolo pellet with a flat head, has evolved (Fig 16). The majority of target marksmen use the wadcutter pellet, and its use in competition is sometimes compulsory. They are available from many makers in tins of 500, and from some specialist firms in packs of 100. In the latter each pellet is individually supported and is thus prevented from sustaining any damage that might impair its accuracy. Naturally such packs are expensive, but many target marksmen feel that such an investment is worthwhile.

HUNTING PATTERNS        17 Hunting pattern pellets

Target marksmen tend to be conservative in their choice of weapons and ammunition, but the hunting fraternity is not so constrained. There are many pellet types in production (Fig 17), from the American 'ash-can', known as the 'dustbin' in the UK, to the new generation of pointed pellets. All have their advocates and there seems to be little conclusive evidence to suggest that one design is more effective than another. Research continues, and there is a nylon waisted pellet under development at the moment. It seems likely that the American calibre of .20 will emerge as the most popular compromise for the hunter, with .177 remaining the exclusive preserve of the target marksman.

**External Ballistics**

From the moment the pellet leaves the barrel to the strike on the target is a fraction of a second, but still long enough to be of vital importance to the accuracy of the shot. The study of that period is a complex science in itself, and something of a closed book to all but the most dedicated marksman. One is merely happy that the bullet strikes the target on the spot aimed for; there is no real need to know why. But the airgunner will not be long in the sport without being involved in the calibre controversy: .22 or .177?

The smaller calibre is .177, and the choice of the target marksman. That this should be so is not simply an accident but based on the ballistics of the smaller pellet. Taking two air rifles of similar design producing around 9ft/lb of muzle energy, the .22 will have a muzzle velocity of 550fps compared with 680fps for the .177. This comes about through the smaller mass of the .177 pellet being propelled faster by the charge of air. Such a high muzzle velocity is not necessary for accuracy over short ranges, and so the designer of the target airweapon can reduce its power and consequently the recoil, achieving a weapon that cocks easily and fires smoothly. The disadvantage of the .177 is that the high muzzle velocity is retarded quickly by the rapid build up of pressure in front of the pellet during its initial flight. Despite the high muzzle velocity, the maximum distance a .177 pellet will travel is only about half that of a .22 when fired from the same type of gun. On the other hand, high muzzle velocity has one advantage for the short range shooter − the initial trajectory is flatter and thus potentially more accurate.

It may seem from the foregoing that there are no real advantages from using a .22 airweapon. This is probably true for the target shooter, but for the hunter the .22 pellet has particular advantages. With its greater projected area the .22 pellet, although travelling with a lower initial velocity, will, on striking its target, give up its kinetic energy more quickly and thus have a greater stopping effect on an animal. This should ensure an effective kill where a similar strike with a .177 pellet would leave only a wounded animal.

Because of its accuracy and high velocity over short ranges, the .177 calibre is the natural choice for the target marksman. If the hunter can be sure of always hitting his prey in a vital spot, the .177 pellet is adequate. For any person not so confident of his marksmanship, the larger calibre should ensure fewer wounded animals in the countryside. In the United Kingdom airgun pellets are available from both Continental and English makers. As a general rule Continental guns are happier with Continental ammunition and English weapons with English pellets. This seems to be because Continental weapons and pellets are made to metric standards while the English adhere to Imperial measure. Theoretically the two systems should produce the same end result, but very wide discrepancies in group size and position have been noted when crossing guns and ammunition from different countries. Best results will be obtained by zeroing a pistol or rifle for a particular type and batch of ammunition and always using the same combination.

## Lead Poisoning

The dangers of lead poisoning would seem to have passed with the Victorian age, but there is a very slight risk to shooters, particularly those who spend long periods of time on indoor ranges. Although there has only been one authenticated case of lead poisoning from shooting – an American pistol instructor who had spent his entire working life on enclosed ranges – the airgunner should take one or two sensible precautions.

Each time an airgunner loads his weapon, he is handling a lead pellet. This contact is not, in itself, dangerous but it does leave a small trace of lead on the fingers. This lead can be conveyed to the mouth, on food, for example, and over a period of time could seriously increase lead levels in the body. So it is wise not to eat while shooting, and one should always wash one's hands after a shoot. A second danger is the possibility of inhaling lead dust which is present wherever lead is broken up – the situation which exists at the 'butts', or target end of a range. An extractor fan or a door which can be opened to ensure a through draught of air will solve this problem. Lead dust in the atmosphere is not a danger to the outdoor shooter, but the hunter should beware of carrying food and pellets in the same pocket, or eating sandwiches with hands covered in lead dust.

## Accessories

SIGHTS

The sole function of the sighting system is to enable a pellet to be directed to hit a place determined by the marksman, which, but for the action of gravity, would be a simple matter of looking along the barrel and firing. The curved path of a bullet – its trajectory – means that in order to hit a particular point, the barrel of the weapon is not necessarily pointing at that particular spot at the moment of firing (Fig 18). Those rare occasions when the barrel is directly aligned

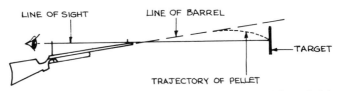

18 A much exaggerated trajectory, line of barrel and line of sight

with the target are given the name 'point blank' range; on all other occasions the line of the barrel is likely to be somewhat above the target axis. But the line of sight of a rifle ideally extends from the shooter's eye through the sights to the centre of the target.

## Basic Sighting Systems

Any sighting system controls a weapon in four directions; up, down, left and right, commonly considered as two pairs and called 'elevation' and 'windage' respectively (Fig 19). In the most simple sighting system, elevation is controlled by aligning the top of the foresight blade with the top of the rearsight. Windage is similarly controlled by centering the foresight in the rearsight notch. The sights illustrated in Figs 20 and 21 are called 'open sights', because they are not enclosed in any way, and are commonly found on pistols and some rifles. There are variations on the basic pattern of

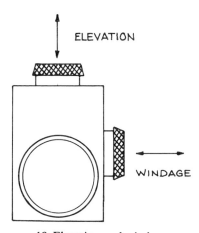

19 Elevation and windage

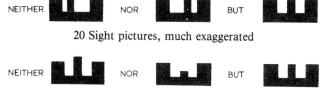

20 Sight pictures, much exaggerated

21 Sight pictures, much exaggerated

22 Bead foresight and V notch rearsight

square blade and notch, as shown in Figs 20 and 21, perhaps the oldest being the bead foresight and V notch backsight used on some hunting rifles (Fig 22).

*Adjustable Sights*

Fixed sights suffer from the disadvantage that they are accurate for one distance only and one condition of wind velocity. When firing over different distances or in varying winds, the marksman will have to 'aim off' in order to hit the target. Provided the amount of correction required is small, this is not an insuperable problem, but having to repeat the exact amount of aim off for each succeeding shot is a considerable handicap, and so adjustable sights are fitted as standard to almost every airweapon. This means that at least the rearsight is adjustable for elevation, using one of a number of methods, which, at its simplest, need be no more than a leaf spring depressed by a fine pitch screw (Fig 23). As the screw is tightened, the rearsight is lowered for short range shooting; loosening the screw raises the sight for longer ranges. The addition of an adjustment for windage can be equally simple, with a small screw pushing or pulling the rearsight notch away from the centre position, depending on the direction and amount of rotation.

The effect on the fall of a pellet of moving the rearsight can be confusing, especially as not all weapon manufacturers use the same notation on their sight adjustment knobs, nor indeed the same direction of rotation for left/right, up/down.

'Positive' adjustment is the usual system favoured by English gun-makers: if the shot is required to fall more to the right, then the sight knob is turned in the direction indicated by 'R', and likewise with the other functions. This is a simple system, and comes naturally to the average marksman.

The 'Corrective' adjustment system is used on some of the finest Continental airweapons, and entails moving the sight knob in the direction of the error. Thus, if a shot falls left, then the knob is rotated in the direction of 'L' (not 'R' as

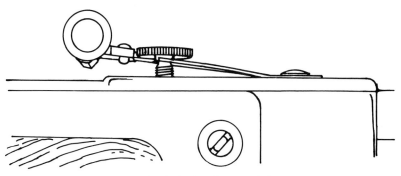

23 Simple leaf spring rearsight

would be the case with positive adjustment). To complicate this system the control knobs bear letters relating to words in the German language: 'L' (links) left, 'R' (rechts) right, 'H' (hoch) high are no problem but 'T' (tief) meaning low must be remembered.

The best advice is to become familiar with one sighting system and stay with it, but if faced with an unknown set of sights, look at the actual physical movement of the rearsight as the elevation and windage knobs are turned. When the rearsight moves up, the shot goes up. When the rearsight moves left, the shot falls left. Sights up, shot up. Sights left, shot left.

### Aperture Sights

The hunter, when not using a telescopic sight, usually uses an open sight as this gives a wider field of view for locating a moving target. The competition rifleman, however, is concerned with a static target which requires a great degree of precision if it is to be hit time and again. The chief aid to achieving this end is the aperture sight, a device which severely restricts the marksman's field of view, but allows very accurate alignment of the rifle with the target.

*Aperture Rearsight* The sighting aperture (Fig 24) is usually adjustable to allow for differing light conditions, the shooter's ideal being an aperture which allows both the

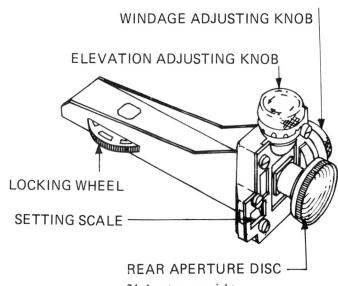

WINDAGE ADJUSTING KNOB

ELEVATION ADJUSTING KNOB

LOCKING WHEEL

SETTING SCALE

REAR APERTURE DISC

24 Aperture rearsight

foresight ring and the aiming mark to appear sharp. It is impossible for the human eye to focus on aiming mark, foresight and rearsight simultaneously, but a small aperture will improve the depth of focus, in the same way that reducing the aperture of a camera improves sharpness over a long distance. There are limits, however, and apertures below 1mm may seriously affect the definition of the aiming mark; judging the correct aperture can only come with experience.

The elevation and windage controls on an aperture sight are fine pitch screws of micrometer precision. As they are turned, a 'click' is audible, and each click represents a fixed amount of displacement of the pellet on the target, the actual amount depending on the standard of the maker. Changes in sight setting can be expressed either by counting the number of 'clicks' in whatever direction, or by the more scientific method of measuring the angles of arc traversed by the rifle. The latter is made possible when one knows what minute of arc is crossed by each click of the sight. The manufacturer usually provides this information (a popular English sight has

'¼ minute clicks'), and the total movement in any direction can be read off micrometer scales on the body of the sight.

All this may seem rather complex but such is the accuracy of target air rifles that each click of a popular German rearsight moves the point of impact by only $\frac{1}{5}$ of the width of one scoring ring at a range of 10m. In practice the competition airgunner who owns his own weapons will not need to agonise over sight changes, as shooting takes place at only two distances, 6yd and 10m, and usually indoors. This means that once the sights have been zeroed for each distance, the difference between the two zeros can be remembered and simply set on the sight before shooting at each distance. Alternatively, and perhaps easier, the number of clicks between the zeros can be counted and used to reset the sights when moving from one distance to another. From then on only small sight adjustments should be necessary, as dictated by changes in lighting conditions on different ranges or other local differences.

*Aperture Foresight* An aperture foresight is a small metal tube, usually referred to as a 'tunnel', into which it is possible

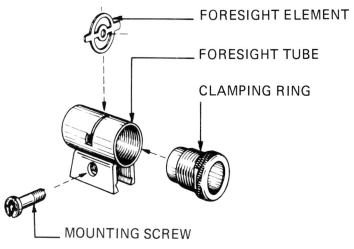

FORESIGHT ELEMENT

FORESIGHT TUBE

CLAMPING RING

MOUNTING SCREW

25 Aperture foresight

to lock one of a number of different interchangeable 'elements' (Fig 25). Before considering the problems of which element to use, an appreciation of what the marksman is trying to achieve is important. The target shooter is concerned, sometimes even obsessed, with his 'sight picture', that is to say, the image he sees when looking at a card through his sighting system. As can be seen from the figure on page 77, the bull is considerably smaller than the aiming mark. In fact, at 10m it is quite impossible to actually see the bull with the naked eye, yet it is quite possible to hit it every time using an aperture sight. This is achieved by maintaining exactly the same sight picture for every shot, and directing the pellet towards the bull by changing the sight *adjustment*, not the *picture*.

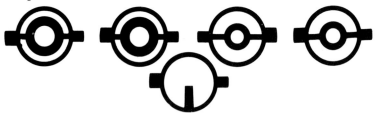

26 Foresight elements

The choice of foresight element (Fig 26) is to the marksman what the choice of float or spinner is to the fisherman; there are many patterns, all with their devoted followers, but none is universally infallible. There is, however, one golden rule to guide a marksman in his choice of foresight element: it is a serious mistake to use a very small element. By their nature, foresight elements restrict the passage of some light, and a small foresight element can distort the image of the aiming mark to such an extent that shots are quite unpredictable. To a certain degree, this effect depends on the level of target illumination, but it is always safer to use a foresight element that allows a fair amount of white to be seen around the aiming mark, rather than an element that fits tightly.

In addition to elements of different shapes, it is also permitted for riflemen to introduce filters into the sighting system. Again this is a matter of personal experience, but some marksmen find that a yellow filter in the rearsight improves the contrast of the sight picture. For those who wear spectacles it is often more satisfactory to fit a corrective lens to the rearsight, although this is not allowed under UIT rules, than to shoot wearing glasses.

Many riflemen find they cannot shoot with both eyes open, nor can they easily close the non-shooting eye without also affecting the sighting eye. This problem can easily be solved, either by wearing an eyepatch, or by the more satisfactory method of adding a special mask to the rearsight. This can be simply a piece of an old target, or a specially made shield.

*Pistol Sights*
Aperture sights are only used on target rifles, the pistoleer being restricted to open sights (Fig 27). The pistol shooter has the same sighting adjustments available to him as the rifle shot, but for the pistol shooter the maintenance of the correct relationship between foresight blade and rearsight notch is vitally important. The actual width of blade and notch adopted will depend on personal preference, but it is usual to use a fairly broad foresight blade, and adjust the rearsight notch to give a clear band of white on either side of the blade. As with rifle sights, it is impossible to indicate a specific choice of pistol sight since much depends on the individual

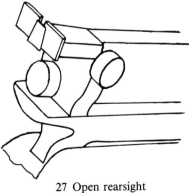

27 Open rearsight

shooter, the distance from the eye to the rearsight (termed 'eye relief'), the distance from rearsight to foresight (the 'sight base') and the conditions on each range.

### Telescopic Sights

The telescopic sight is theoretically the perfect sight. Its use is allowed in only one type of competition – moving target – but for the hunter it is the preferred sight. At its most basic, a 'scope sight' is a simple telescope with a reticle inserted in the path of the light rays in such a position that both the reticle and the target can be seen simultaneously in sharp focus. Usually a system of knobs is provided to adjust the sight for elevation and windage, and adjustable clamps to mount the sight on different rifles. Telescopic sights are most often seen on rifles, but some pistol scopes are made and sometimes used by hunters who use air pistols on small game. The optical construction of rifle and pistol scopes is quite different, and they cannot be used interchangeably, simply because of the much greater eye relief required of the pistol scope.

With any telescopic sight there are two factors of primary importance: magnification and light gathering power. A high magnification is not usually as desirable as it may at first seem. Any magnification over 8× will so accentuate a marksman's natural wobble that he may hesitate to press the trigger. In time, every shooter learns to cope with some unsteadiness, but most users of telescopic sights settle for a lower magnification, around 4×.

The light gathering power of a telescope is controlled by its magnification and the physical size of the front lens of the scope. A working guide can be found by dividing the diameter (in mm) of the forward lens by the magnification. Thus 4× magnification with an objective lens of 20mm would have a factor of 5. The lower the number, the darker will be the picture seen through the scope. A telescopic sight with a factor of less than 3 is probably best avoided as its prolonged use could result in eye-strain. This light gathering factor is usually referred to as the 'Exit Pupil'.

The reticle, the 'cross hairs' familiar from many a spy film, is the device for directing the rifle onto the target. The principle is well known, and from the simple crossed vertical and horizontal lines, reticles are available in many patterns, one manufacturer offering seven different types. The choice of reticle is one of personal preference; some patterns lend themselves to shooting at moving targets, others are better employed on static marks, while there is one type of sight with two independently adjustable reticles, designed specifically for the running boar competition.

CLOTHING FOR SHOOTERS

It may seem surprising that in addition to weapons, marksmen require shooting clothing, but it is true that most successful shots, riflemen in particular, wear some highly specialised garments.

*Shooting Jackets*

The jacket is probably the most important item of clothing that a target rifleman wears. Under international rules padding is allowed on the elbows, the back of the left upper arm, and the right shoulder, in the case of a right-handed rifleman.

While all this is not strictly necessary for the air rifleman who always shoots standing, any airgunner purchasing a special shooting jacket is well advised to obtain a type that will be suitable also for .22 cartridge weapons, ready for the time when the air rifleman decides to try his hand at the other discipline. The principle advantage of a jacket is that it provides some support for the rifleman in the standing position. Consequently a shooting jacket should be made of leather or some similar supple but non-elastic material, be of tough construction to add support to the shoulders and with the permitted padding on shoulder, arm and elbows.

In the past riflemen have been able to press into service any old jacket or wind-cheater as a shooting jacket, and the organisers of many of today's competitions are not over strict in enforcing the rules on clothing. Nevertheless, the rules laid down by the UIT are strict and specific, and any rifleman intending to shoot in National or International meetings must abide by them. In the matter of clothing, the 1981 UIT rules specify the following points which are applicable to air rifle shooters:

a) The shooting jacket may only be fastened by non-adjustable means. The jacket may not overlap more than 10cm at the closure. The jacket must hang loosely on the wearer and to determine this the jacket must be capable of being overlapped beyond the normal closure by at least 7cm.

b) Padding is permitted at the shooting shoulder, on the back of the non-shooting upper arm, and on both elbows, provided that the thickness of the jacket does not exceed 10mm single thickness, or 20mm double thickness.

These rules may seem somewhat complicated, but any rifleman buying a shooting jacket from a reputable maker can expect that a jacket specifically described as 'a UIT jacket' will comply with all the rules.

*Shooting Gloves*

In whatever position a target rifle is fired, prone, kneeling or standing, the hand supporting the rifle is under considerable strain. This can be extreme in the course of a UIT match, and so most riflemen use a glove on their non-trigger hand to give protection and some support (Fig 28). There are strict rules governing the length of such a glove (it may not extend beyond the wrist) and be of regulation thickness. Additionally, the glove should not cramp the fingers, and to this end a mitt, in which the fingers are maintained together in one pouch as opposed to the individual finger stalls of a glove, may offer greater comfort (Fig 29). Shooting gloves and mitts are available through gun shops and the NSRA, and are well worth spending money on.

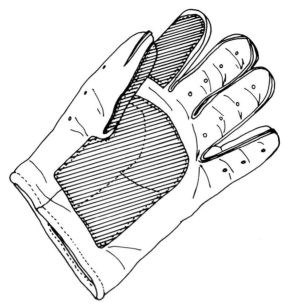

28 Shooting glove

29 Shooting mitt

30 Shooting boot

*Shooting Shoes*
This item is by no means a necessity for good shooting, but it is noticeable that many top ranking shooters do wear special footwear. UIT regulations restrict the size and thickness of shoes and a pair of specially built shooting shoes can be quite an expensive purchase. However, it is probably a good idea to acquire a stout pair of sporting shoes with non-marking composition soles, as many airweapon competitions take place in leisure centres where there are strict rules about the footwear that may be worn in the sports halls.

Contrary to what was considered essential in the past, strong stiff boots to give support to the ankles are not necessary — many of the top shooters use soft shoes or boots with soft sides and flexible soles. However, a firm sole is essential and should not be too 'springy', as in some training shoes currently available for jogging. A flat sole without a separate heel is considered beneficial (Fig 30). When choosing a boot or shoe, ensure that it complies with the UIT rules, otherwise when you turn up for a competition you will be requested to use shoes which do comply and the change could be disastrous to your shooting.

1 Weihrauch HW35 rifle with Tasco 2.5 × 32 'scope

2 BSA Mercury S with Tasco 4 × 32 'scope

3 BSA Meteor

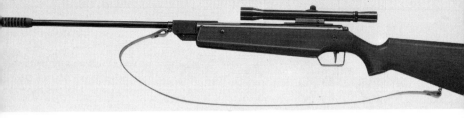

4 Original 45S with 4 × 20 'scope

5 Original 45 with Viking 'scope

6 Webley Vulcan with Tasco 'scope

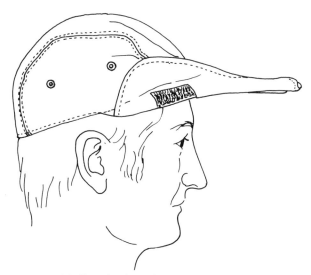

31 Shooting hat with long peak

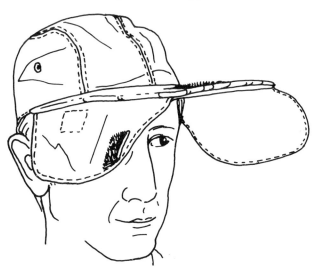

32 Shooting hat with side flaps extended

## Hats

Some marksmen shoot bareheaded, many wear hats. A special shooting hat with a long peak and side flaps can reduce external distractions, such as movement on adjacent firing points or glare from lights, and can prevent hair from slipping into one's eyes during shooting (Figs 31 and 32). The use of a hat is purely a matter of personal preference, and if wearing one helps an individual's concentration when on the firing point, then it is to be recommended.

33 Ear muffs

*Hearing Protectors*

The use of some form of ear muffs or plugs is essential for those involved in shooting with cartridge firearms. There is no question that prolonged exposure to firearms detonations, particularly indoors, ruins hearing. By contrast the loudest noise on an airgun range is probably the range officer coughing, but many airweapons shooters still use ear muffs. This is usually for two reasons: in the first place ear muffs do deaden all other distracting sounds, and if this helps concentration then ear muffs should be worn. In the second place, many airweapon shooters also shoot cartridge weapons as an additional hobby, and it can help both disciplines if the marksman wears the same clothing for each, thus always keeping a known set of conditions. Needless to say many international marksmen use ear muffs for cartridge shooting, and no protection when firing airweapons.

Hearing protectors fall into two types: plugs and muffs (Fig 33). Plugs usually fit into the ear, and can be anything from an old .38 cartridge case (not to be recommended) through cottonwool to special sonic valves. I have tried most types and found them effective but uncomfortable. Muffs, on the other hand, fit over the ears, and are most effective, but can be hot in prolonged use. They can also be a problem if the shooter wears glasses with heavy earpieces, but on the whole I have found them more satisfactory than plugs. The best muffs are the sort issued to ground crew who work in the vicinity of jet engines, but there are many patterns available and a purchaser should consider carefully whether he will want ear defenders solely for airweapon shooting or may later extend his interest to cartridge weapons.

## Clothing for Pistol Shooters

The pistol shooter can function without any special clothing at all. Indeed this is one of the delights of being a pistol marksman, never more appreciated than in a hot drill hall. But in practise most pistol shots have some items of special clothing, be they spectacles, ear muffs, shoes or special jackets designed to support the non-shooting hand. Most airweapon shooting takes place indoors, so exposure to weather is not a general hazard. Some matches, however, are held outdoors or in unheated premises, and during winter months, the cold can cause severe problems for the pistol shot. To combat such conditions special quilted pistol waistcoats are available, and any pistoleer who expects to shoot outdoors regularly should practise shooting in such a waistcoat or in any jacket that he prefers as weather protection. Generally, outdoor firing points are roofed and enclosed as protection against rain, but cold wind inevitably circulates round the firing points, and can be a considerable handicap for the unprepared.

SHOOTING GLASSES

As considered briefly earlier in this chapter, closing the non-sighting eye can be a major problem for some people. The modern theory is to shoot with both eyes open, thus relaxing the eye muscles equally, and using mental concentration to select the correct sight picture. This is a practical impossibility for many people, and so various forms of eyeshields are used. Specialist shooting glasses are designed to be completely adjustable and to carry any occluders, black patches, prescription lenses and orthopters in whatever position they may be required. Complete adjustability of lenses is desirable as normal spectacles seldom sit on the face in exactly the right place for all shooting positions. The use of shooting spectacles tends to be more common among pistol shooters than riflemen. This is because the rifle rearsight, with its variable aperture and facility for the addition of an eyeshield over the non-shooting eye is able to accommodate more differences in visual acuity than the very basic open sights of the pistol. As it is impossible for the pistoleer to keep aiming mark, backsight and foresight in focus simultaneously, and any shift in focus changes the perceived size of all three, the pistol marksman often uses an orthopter, or variable iris, over his shooting eye.

This device functions in exactly the same way as the variable aperture rearsight on the rifle in improving the depth of focus and ensuring that the head is in the same position from shot to shot. Pistol irises can be bought either as devices to be attached by suction cup to an existing pair of spectacles, or as a separate component to attach to shooting spectacle frames (Fig 34).

34 Pistol iris for shooting glasses

The non-shooting eye should, ideally, receive the same amount of light as the shooting eye, hence the suggestion of shooting with both eyes open. Clearly to have one eye receiving no light, while the other receives a bright signal, will cause strain; balancing the two inputs, while preventing the non-shooting eye from receiving an image, leads to some interesting devices. Some marksmen put small circular patches over their spectacle lenses, others use occluders of opalescent material while yet others use pieces of old target secured by a hat or hairband. The solutions are innumerable, and the best advice is to find out what suits you and stick to it.

SPOTTING TELESCOPES

As distinct from telescopic sights, spotting scopes are allowed and are used to observe the position of the shot hole on the card. Spotting telescopes are not strictly necessary for airweapon shooting on advanced ranges or in major competitions as such ranges are equipped with devices that automatically return the card to the firer, and he can thus see the value and position of the shot. However, automatic target changers are not universal, and some marksmen find them distracting and prefer to observe their shots without moving the target. A spotting telescope is essential for target shooting with firearms, and so any airweapon shooter contemplating the purchase of a spotting scope is well advised to buy one that will serve for all forms of shooting.

There are a number of spotting telescopes available, and as they tend to be expensive it is wise to be sure of exactly what one wants. Generally, a spotting telescope should have a magnification of $20\times$ to $30\times$ (a zoom scope can be a good buy) and exit pupil (diameter of front lens in mm divided by magnification) of not less than 2.5–3mm and, most important of all, be capable of focusing down to the shortest distance at which one expects to shoot. For an airweapon shooter this means at least 10m and possibly even 6yd, implying a closeness of focus not usually found on standard telescopes.

Some modern spotting telescopes are supplied with interchangeable eyepieces to allow a variation in magnification, and angled eyepieces to facilitate spotting without too much movement of one's firing position. In addition to a telescope, the marksman will need some form of tripod to support the scope. This can be a simple photographic tripod or a specially made device with a precision head and supporting legs, often costing a considerable sum. Such a tripod and telescope will be of most benefit to the keen marksman who follows other disciplines in addition to airweapons shooting, but for the casual, airweapons only marksman, a pair of 8 × 30 binnoculars, or even a monocular, will suffice.

# 4 The Sport of Target Shooting

It is not generally appreciated that target shooting, taken in all its forms, is the second largest participator sport in Britain. (Angling is the first.) Naturally such a widely practised pastime needs internationally recognised bodies to regulate it, and the shooting disciplines are no exception. The novice airgunner will not be long in the sport before he hears of the N.S.R.A., N.A.R.P.A, 'UIT' rules and occasionally, from an old timer, the ISU. Taken in order the initials stand for National Small-Bore Rifle Association, National Air Rifle & Pistol Association, Union International de Tir, and International Shooting Union.

**National Small-Bore Rifle Association**
The NSRA is the most important British authority over all forms of small bore (.22 cartridge and airweapons) shooting and is recognised internationally as the body responsible for holding national championship meetings. Every shooter who wishes to take part in national or international competitions

must either be an individual member of the NSRA himself or associated via his club. The NSRA publishes bimonthly an official journal called *The Rifleman*, which is circulated to all members and affiliated clubs, and contains information on past successes, forthcoming meetings, official notices, readers' letters and articles on shooting topics. Although the title National Small-Bore Rifle Association dates only from 1947, the Association can look back to the turn of the century for its roots. In 1899 Britain declared war on the Boers of South Africa, and found, much to public dismay, that the British Army was no match for the Afrikaaners. The reverses suffered by the expeditionary forces were attributed to the great accuracy of Boer marksmanship, and a movement took shape in Britain with the aim of encouraging all men to learn to shoot.

In 1900 Lt V.D.O. Noble announced the formation of the British Rifle League, and in 1901 Major-General C.E. Luard instigated a meeting at which the Society of Working Men's Rifle Clubs was formed. By 1903 the two associations had merged and adopted the title of The Society of Miniature Rifle Clubs, the word 'miniature' referring to the calibre (.22) used, as distinct from full-bore (.303) shooting, then, as now, governed by the National Rifle Association.

The new society had as its Committee Chairman Major Luard and the Duke of Norfolk as Chairman of the Council. Field-Marshal Earl Roberts, Commander-in-Chief of the Army and himself a veteran of the Boer War, accepted the presidency of the new society, but did not take up the post until after retirement from the Army in 1904. He was an enthusiastic and effective president, so much so that he is remembered to this day. The premier small-bore rifle event, shot annually, is the Earl Roberts Memorial Challenge Cup, and a facsimile of his signature appears on every target issued by the NSRA, whose headquarters is at Lord Roberts House, Bisley in Surrey.

**National Air Rifle & Pistol Association**

Airweapon shooting in Britain has had a solid base of support in the Midlands since early in this century. The first team airweapon shoot in Britain is believed to have taken place in 1902, when a group of farmers competed against each other in Bridgnorth, Shropshire, a town which now houses the headquarters of NARPA. World War II caused a decline in target airgun shooting which was not reversed until the middle 1950s, and in Britain the sport emerged as two separate types of competitions: those fired at 10m distance in accordance with European practice, and those fired at 6yd — the original 'English' distance. The 6yd clubs tended to be located in the Midlands, where the Birmingham Small-Arms Company had done much to encourage the sport, but the shorter range was in danger of being eclipsed by the international distance of 10m. In 1970 a small number of 6yd league clubs decided to form the Air Rifle Clubs Association (ARCA), to promote 6yd airweapon shooting as they had recognised that the NSRA was principally concerned with 10m shooting. In 1974 ARCA became NARPA (National Air Rifle & Pistol Association), the better to reflect the Association's wider field of activities, which runs two major league competitions a year, an annual shoulder-to-shoulder final and publishes a bimonthly magazine called *Target*. At the present time NARPA and the NSRA use targets of different dimensions for 6yd shooting, but as the two associations are working closely together it is to be hoped that some form of standardisation will emerge.

In addition to promoting shooting at paper targets, NARPA is involved in bell target shooting. This is a somewhat specialised type of shooting, fired either on a shoulder-to-shoulder basis or as a postal league, at a metal target so arranged that a bell rings when a bull is scored. This form of competition dates from the early 1900s when bicycle bells were used as targets.

### Union Internationale de Tir (UIT)

The International Shooting Union (in abbreviated form UIT from the French title and not ISU from the English translation, to avoid confusion with the International Skating Union) is the world governing body for all forms of amateur competitive shooting with guns. The UIT was formed in 1907, with Great Britain as a founder member. Its headquarters are located in Munich, and controlled by a Secretary General. The organisation has a President, three Vice-Presidents, and three elected members who together with the Director-General and the Chairman of the technical committee, make up the Executive Committee, which meets twice a year. Overall policy decisions are taken by the Administrative Council, an assembly of dignitaries from the various sections, committees, and international confederations that make up the UIT.

The General Assembly meets every two years, usually at the venue of a World Championship or an Olympic Games, and consists of the representatives of over seventy nations. Simultaneous translation of the proceedings into five languages is provided, and the Assembly deals with an agenda not unlike that of the Annual General Meeting of any humble rifle club. The average airweapon shooter is unlikely to have much contact with the UIT, except on those occasions when he shoots a UIT course of fire, usually at an open meeting. In the normal course of club shooting, the shooter is more likely to find himself competing under local or national rules.

**Target Types**
There are six main types of airweapon target currently in use in Britain, four issued by the NSRA and two by NARPA. It is likely that both associations will agree on a standard 6yd target, which will reduce the number of target types currently available by two.

*NSRA Targets*

37 NSRA 10m rifle target, type Air 3, actual size

38 NSRA 6yd rifle target, type Air 7, actual size

39 NSRA 10m pistol target, type Air 4, actual size

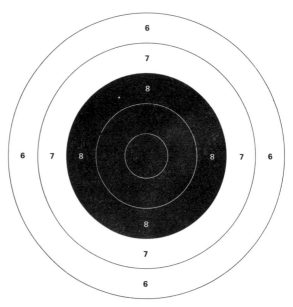

40 NSRA 6yd pistol target, type Air 6, actual size

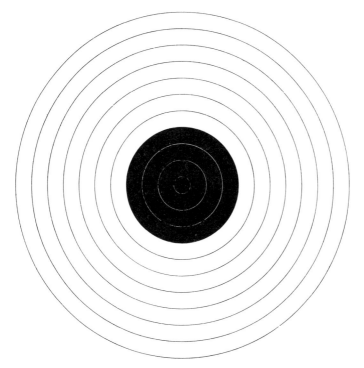

41 Proposed new combined NSRA and NARPA 6yd pistol target, Air 8.

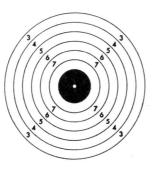

42 NARPA 6yd rifle target

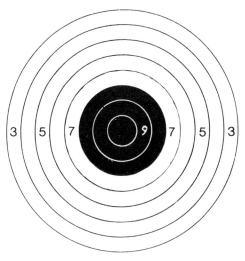

43 NARPA 6yd pistol target

**Courses of Fire**

Every shooting competition consists of a number of scoring shots and a number of non-scoring 'sighters' fired at a stipulated distance, usually within a given time limit. Such a procedure is called a course of fire, and may follow a pattern laid down by a national or international governing body, or be simply decided upon by a committee organising a local shoot. The most familiar course of fire is the UIT 10m match, which for rifle consists of unlimited sighters and 60 scoring shots, fired in 2¼ hours. The sighters are taken before starting the competition cards, and are fired on separate, specially designated targets. At the end of the course all cards, sighters as well as match cards, are handed in for scoring. This is a strenuous and lengthy match, and most club competitions are of up to 10 sighters and 20 shots to count being fired in about half an hour, or the old UIT course of 10 sighters and 40 scoring shots in 1½ hours. Courses of fire vary immensely and it ought to go without saying that the shooter must be sure of the match conditions before starting to fire.

**Bell Target Shooting**

From the early sport of shooting at bicycle bells, a modern descendant has emerged − bell target shooting. This form of competition enjoys its greatest popularity in the British Midlands, being fired either as a shoulder-to-shoulder or postal league competition on both individual and team basis. The target (Fig 44) consists of a steel plate having a central hole of .375in diameter, around which are engraved four concentric scoring rings. In operation, the target face is coated with non drying white paint, the purpose of which is to indicate the point of impact of any shots that do not pass through the central hole; shots passing cleanly through the hole trip a mechanism which causes a bell to ring and a flag bearing the figure 5 to appear in the target box.

This indicates the maximum score of 5 points, and is recorded as such on a match card. Shots falling outside the 5 ring are scored visually and entered on the card, following which the target face is painted over, making ready for the next shot. To guarantee accuracy, scoring is carried out by

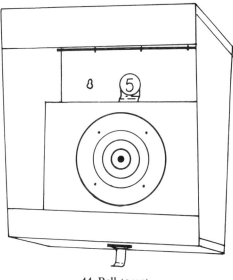

44 Bell target

both a marker and a checker, with an appeal to a third person in the event of disputed shots. Bell targets are fired at from a distance of 6yd, and courses of fire vary between 10 and 40 shots, depending on local rules. A national league is run by NARPA, but essentially bell target shooting has changed little from the early years of this century when shooters fired at targets illuminated by gas-light.

### An Airweapon's Range
Of course, any piece of ground with a tin can at one end and a rifleman at the other can be called a range, but such an arrangement is usually unsatisfactory and dangerous. Airgun pellets can ricochet from the ground − from stones and the like − with enough force to hurt someone, including the rifleman who discharged the shot in the first place. So it is a sensible idea to arrange some form of pellet trap. At its simplest this need be no more than a canvas, or heavy

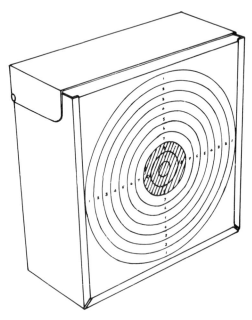

45 Pellet catcher

7 Webley Hurricane pistol

8 Crossman 1377 pistol

9 Walther LGR target rifle

10 Feinwerkbau 300SU target rifle

11 Original 75HV target rifle

material sheet or rug suspended loosely behind the target area. This will absorb the energy of the pellet and deposit it harmlessly on the ground. A sheet has the advantage that it will effectively cover a wide area, and can be used as a backing to a row of tin cans, coins, or whatever.

After a time the novice airgunner usually improves in accuracy and so searches for a more demanding target, quite often a paper target of some description, whose scoring rings allow a method of evaluating and comparing performance. Such a target, either home-made or of the official variety, can still be fixed in front of a simple rag backstop but it is usually more convenient to slot the target into a special pellet catcher (Fig 45). Pellet catchers are available commercially for only a few pounds, but a suitable trap can be home-made very easily. Principally, such a trap consists of a steel plate of at least 16 gauge held at 45 degrees in a box somewhat larger than the targets it is to hold. Cards are secured in front of the open side of the trap either in channels or with small clips, pellets passing through the cards, hitting the angled steel plate and falling harmlessly into the bottom of the box, to be emptied later.

There are a number of novel variations on the basic pellet trap commercially available, ranging from falling levers and bell targets to moving target ranges. So for individual practise an inexpensive pellet catcher set in a suitably safe position indoors or out, with the chosen range carefully measured and a table conveniently placed to carry pellets, weapon and telescope will suffice admirably. The location for such a range can be in the garden, garage or down a long corridor inside a house. I am sure I am not the only shooter who fires from the bathroom down a corridor into a box room, but such an arrangement, though effective, needs real domestic harmony.

## A Club Range

Clearly a single pellet trap is not suitable for a club, or indeed any occasion where a number of people wish to shoot at one time, but with a little ingenuity it can be adapted. A 6yd range is simpler to construct than a 10m range, if only because the hall, or space required need only be 25ft long by about 3ft wide for each firing point. A Scout hut, or similar building could be used for a 6yd range with the provision of some dismountable frames and folding tables; the advantage of such a system being that the hall could quickly revert to its original use when the range was not being used.

The first consideration in using a social hall as a range is, of course, that the chance of pellets damaging fixtures and fittings must be eliminated. This can be achieved by the rigid enforcement of safety rules and the provision of an adequate backstop. With airweapon shooting, the beginner tends to miss the target, and thus the pellet catcher, fairly often, while the expert would be devastated to miss either. So while a small sheet of steel behind each target would be sufficient on a range to be used only by experts, the novice requires greater protection. This can be achieved by mounting the pellet catchers on screens of ¾in plywood as large as space permits. Such a backstop can be made in sections, dismountable for storage, and suitable nails or screws provided on which to hang pellet traps. The target centres should be 5ft from the floor, 3ft apart and in a line parallel to the firing line, indicated by a thick line or tape on the floor 18ft from the target faces. This line is so arranged that the shooter's foot must not encroach upon it at all, and it is convenient to place tables on the target side of the line to act as loading tables (Fig 46).

Illumination on the range is important, and it is customary to arrange soft overall light with individual lighting on each target. This can be a small fluorescent light, a flood light or an ordinary bulb, shielded against strikes by pellets.

Naturally, safety precautions are paramount and it is essential that on any temporary range, it be made impossible for shooters, spectators or casual visitors to wander behind the targets or in front of the guns. Shooting should be controlled by a range officer who gives the commands to commence and cease fire, ensures that all weapons are

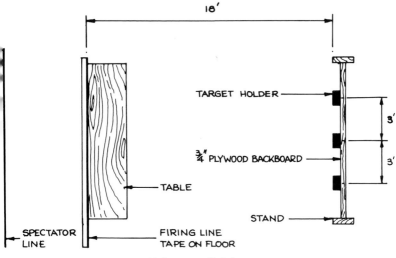

46 Layout of club range

unloaded and placed on the shooting tables before anyone goes forward to change the targets, and that no weapon is even touched when people are in front of the firing point.

The provision of a 10m range is rather more difficult as a building of some 45–50ft length is required. Such buildings can be found, but if the range is worked on the simple principles described above, the necessity for all shooters to cease fire before cards can be changed will quickly become tiresome. That this should be more of a problem at 10m than 6yd comes about from the differing nature of the short- and long-range competitions. At 6yd the competitor will not often be firing more than 20 shots during one detail, but at 10m the UIT course requires up to 15 sighting and 60 scoring shots to be fired in a period of 2¼ hours. Clearly different marksmen shoot at different rates, and since no more than 5 shots are usually fired on each target, waiting for a number of competitors to finish their five shots before the targets could be changed would completely destroy the rhythm of the match. In fact such disturbance is not permitted under UIT rules and so systems are introduced that enable the shot card to be returned to the shooter by mechanical means.

THE AUTOMATIC TARGET CHANGER

A form of automatic target changer has been in use at Bisley for many years, being no more than a target holder running on rails and pulled by an endless wire operated by a hand wheel at the firing point.

A similar system can be used on an airweapons' range, but the best solution is the provision of an electrically operated changer (Fig 47). There are several types available, but the basic system is similar in all. At the firing point is the control box with direction switches, on/off switch and the driving motor. The target is carried by a light-weight holder which runs on two nylon threads stretched between the control box

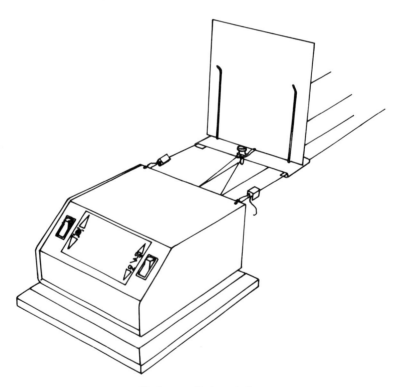

47 Automatic target changer

and the steel plate which acts as a pellet stop. Motive power is carried to the target holder by an additional nylon thread which is attached to the holder and travels round the motor driven pulley wheel at the control box and another at the pellet stop. Direction of travel is selected by pressing the appropriate control switch, and the motor cuts out automatically when the target holder contacts the pellet stop. Thus the equipment can be used at any shooting distance simply by adjusting the position of the pellet stop and ensuring that the supporting and driving lines are at the right tension.

Automatic target changers are quite expensive and do take a little time to set up, so they are generally found in use on custom-built airweapon ranges where they can be left permanently erected or in halls which have been hired for a championship meeting.

### A PERMANENT AIRWEAPONS RANGE

As the members of small-bore rifle clubs became interested in airweapon shooting, conversions of various sorts were carried out to existing ranges. Airweapon shooting is carried out in the standing position whereas rifle shooting in Britain has traditionally been in the prone position — lying on the stomach. This form of shooting requires targets close to the ground, and needs only a narrow aperture along the firing point through which to shoot. Adapting such an indoor range to the standing position can require a fair amount of conversion work, and any adaptation of an existing range can only be an unsatisfactory compromise as shooters will still have to go forward from the firing point to change targets, with consequent interruption to shooting. Where the range will not be used by any marksmen other than airweapon shooters, automatic target changers can be installed, but these devices cannot be left in position if the range is also used by, for example, .22 cartridge riflemen. There comes a time with any rifle or pistol club whose members are also keen airweapon shooters, when the pressure on the existing range facilities forces a decision to build an additional range, solely for airweapon shooting.

The construction of such a range will depend on the talent and enthusiasm of the members, the amount of money that can be raised locally or through grants, and any existing buildings that can be converted; but it is possible to construct an indoor 10m range completely from scratch and with only volunteers' help in a few months. I speak from experience as the members of my club, Tunbridge Wells & St Peters, under the driving leadership of a very determined air rifleman, shifted 50 tons of earth, erected a building 50ft by 18ft, roofed it, installed automatic ventilation and heating and finally six automatic target changers in under four months. The range was officially opened by Gold Medalist Malcolm Cooper, and has proved by its great popularity to have been well worth the money and effort invested in it.

**Starting an Airweapon Club**
There cannot be many towns in Britain without a small-bore rifle or pistol club in the vicinity, but for those keen airweapon shooters who cannot find a range, or for groups of people wishing to form their own teams, their remains the possibility of forming one's own club. Essentially it is not difficult, but it will require dedication, some money, and most important of all, premises. A meeting of interested parties should be called and a number of officers must be elected, at least a Treasurer, Secretary and Captain. Any club that is going to prosper will need a constitution, a document that sets out the clubs aims, the powers of the committee and general rules for members' guidance. While such a document can be drawn up by members, it is probably better to adopt a standard constitution, such as the model offered by the NSRA, adapting it by majority vote to suit local conditions.

While a constitution is really a long-term safeguard, the initial success of a club is likely to hinge on the availability of money and premises. The size of the premises required will depend on whether a club is going to shoot 6yd only or 6yd and 10m. Personally, I suspect that most airweapon shooters will want to be able to shoot, if only occasionally, at 10m and the provision of this distance will be essential if a club is to prosper in the long term. I have fired on many strange 10m ranges, including one beside the swimming pool of a luxury hotel, and it seems that if the spirit is there, a range will be found.

Finance is always a problem, and every club tries to strike its own balance between subscriptions, range fees and fund-raising activities. For a new club it is probably an idea for the original members to personally loan the club enough money to cover foundation expenses, and to recoup the loan from subsequent membership dues. Additionally, members may have or can make bits and pieces of equipment that can be given to the club — pellet catchers and the like — which will reduce initial expenditure.

Before the club members begin to shoot, rules must be posted in a prominent place, and, if possible, circulated personally to each member. It cannot be over-emphasised that the relative freedom from legal restrictions that airweapon shooters enjoy, depends to the largest degree on the safe operation of the sport. The first and greatest responsibility of the captain and committee of a club is range safety, and no other consideration must overrule this. The provision of adequate insurance cover for a club is also essential, but must only be regarded as a sensible precaution and not as a substitute for vigilance.

As a club grows in strength, members will wish to compete more widely, and to this end affiliation to one of the national bodies will be essential, allowing members to compete in national postal league competitions.

## Legal Matters

At the time of writing, British owners of most airweapons do not require Firearm Certificates. The exceptions are those air rifles producing a muzzle energy of more than 12ft lb, air pistols of a muzzle energy of 6ft lb and all airweapons powered by $CO_2$. In practice, manufacturers ensure that their airguns do not exceed these limits, but it is wise to be wary of 'pump up' airweapons, as this design can often allow illegal levels of muzzle energy to be achieved. It is unlikely that a reputable dealer would knowingly sell an illegal weapon to a customer, and only the unwise would tamper with an airgun in an endeavour to increase its power. There are currently no restrictions on airweapons in the United States, and that condition is likely to remain for the foreseeable future.

There are in Britain a number of restrictions currently in force affecting the use of airweapons, and the main points are summarised as follows:

Under the age of 14 a person
   a) May not own or hire an airweapon.
   b) May not have an airweapon in a public place, unless supervised by a person over 21, and unless the weapon be unloaded and securely covered.
   c) May only use an airweapon under the supervision of a person over 21, provided that any missile discharged from the weapon does not travel beyond the premises on which the air rifle or pistol is being used.

Over the age of 14 but under 17, a person
   a) May not purchase or hire an airweapon, but may receive one as a gift or on loan.
   b) May not have an air rifle in a public place unless the weapon is covered in a manner that prevents it being fired, and may not have an air pistol in a public place at any time.

General Rules
   a) Airweapons must not be carried loaded in public places.

b) The permission of the owner or occupier is required to have an airweapon on any private land — trespassing with an airweapon is an offence.

c) A person of any age may use an airweapon on an approved range, or an airweapons only range, or in a shooting gallery.

# PART 2

# 5 An Introduction to Target Shooting

Although the majority of airgun shooters are enthusiasts who shoot at tin cans and the like, as well as those who use their guns for vermin control, there is a growing number who prefer to shoot competitively at targets. Target shooting is now so popular that it is being introduced into the Olympic Games programme as one of the events with a world following that exceeds many other sports. There is already a World Championship which takes place every two years as well as European Championships, Pan American Championships and Asian Championships. There are events for men, ladies and juniors although there is very little difference in the winning standards. The training and effort necessary to win an international event is considerable and equals that of an athlete preparing for his events, even though the athletic event may be primarily physical whereas the shooter's is mental. It is interesting to compare the difference between the athlete and shooter. With an athlete all his energy goes into a physical activity which can be aided by the adrenalin which is produced whenever he takes part in competition. The fact that he is in direct competition with another athlete whom he can see and aim at beating can produce performances which surpass his training achievements. The shooter, on the other hand, is in his own world standing alongside perhaps up to a hundred other shooters on the firing line, striving to maintain steadiness against the competition nerves which are threatening every shot which he fires. The adrenalin which gives a big boost to the athlete can ruin a shooter's score unless it is held in full control, and although there are benefits, such as a heightened awareness and quicker reactions, most shooters perform better during training and in lesser competitions. The athlete's competition nerves are the most severe at the start of the event and disappear once he starts running but a shooter can have these 'butterflies' on every one of his sixty shots. Mental training is now seen as one of the most important tasks for a shooter to carry out in order to minimise the differences between his training and competition scores.

As well as the mental training, it is recognised that even for an event like shooting, where most of the marksman's efforts are going into keeping perfectly still, physical training is necessary. This does not mean that the shooter must be a muscle bound strongman to hold the rifle or pistol steady by physical strength, but that he must be fit so that his body and mind are in good co-ordination and healthy. As is often said, 'a healthy body gives a healthy mind'.

In order to be successful an athlete must practice his event as often as he can which will entail many hours of running, jumping or throwing depending on his specialisation. The shooter must do the same. Although it may appear easy to the onlooker, the training of the mind and body to achieve perfect stillness and co-ordination requires many hours of training each week. The act of firing the shot requires a perfect technique for a number of activities that must be brought together as an integrated whole which will see the shot hit the centre of the target. The firing of a single 10 is not the object of the training, but the firing of many 10s consistently which will build up the winning score. In fact the winning scores in both the rifle and pistol events will consist of at least 75 per cent of the pellets landing in the 10 whilst the remainder are in the 9 ring. If you miss the 9 then you will need more than 75 per cent of 10s. From these requirements, one can see that consistency is the order of the day and that the shooter must strive throughout the competition to avoid stray shots which would ruin an otherwise first-class score.

Having introduced the physical and mental problems which can beset a shooter, we must not forget the equipment.

Unless the gun and pellets are capable of consistently shooting 10s, much of a shooter's efforts will be wasted. Only top quality guns from reputable manufacturers are used at championship level, and the pellets must be specially selected to give satisfactory accuracy and consistency.

In order to progress quickly and to reach one's limit of performance, the shooter, like the successful athlete, must produce a programme of work with goals to be reached at each phase, and he must analyse his work constantly to weed out weaknesses and to enforce his strong points. Whether the shooter succeeds in the end will depend on his own goals, his determination to win, hard work, and his natural abilities.

All of this may sound a bit off-putting to the newcomer but it need not be because not everyone wants to achieve such high goals and many are quite content to visit the club once a week purely for the fun and social aspects. In fact most clubs have only one or two really determined shooters who want to reach the top rank. Nevertheless the ordinary club member should gain a better idea of what is involved in shooting and the information contained in these chapters may enable him to shoot a little better.

# 6 Target Rifle Shooting

**Eyesight**

In order to be able to discriminate the fine detail of a sight picture the eye must have fine visual acuity. The person with normal vision is said to have eyes which can discriminate a test object which subtends an angle of one minute of arc. This is considered to be adequate for target shooting and any shooter who does not have adequate eyesight should visit an optician to obtain a corrective lens. The fact that one must use a corrective lens does not prevent a shooter from achieving international success as many international shooters use spectacles. Special shooting spectacle frames can be obtained which have a lens holder which can be adjusted to ensure that the optical centre of the lens is in the correct position when aiming through the sights. If standard spectacle frames were used, the lens could not easily be adjusted to look through the optical axis whilst looking through the sights. However, if the cost of these shooting glasses is too great, then an ordinary pair could be improved by the use of plasticine/modelling clay on the bridge to line up the centre with the rear sight.

Even though some shooters have excellent eyesight, the characteristics of the human eye vary from person to person and the use of different size rearsight and foresight apertures must be tried in order to choose the optimum sizes which give visual clarity between the aiming mark and white target when viewed through the sights. Different colour filters for the rearsight can also be tried to obtain satisfactory definition of the sight picture. What works for one shooter does not necessarily work for another and the combination could change under different light conditions.

12 Original 10 target pistol

13 Feinwerkbau 65 target pistol

14 The indoor 10m range built by the members of Tunbridge Wells and St Peter's Club

15 A competitor weighing his
pistol during checking in
procedure at the National
Championships

16 Typical selection of medals
from airweapon matches
including World Championsh

To avoid fatigue, both eyes should be kept open whilst aiming as this is how they were designed to operate. Closing one eye will put a strain on the other after a short time and cause a fall in performance when this is carried out over an extended period of time. Some shooters can keep both eyes open without the eye which is not doing the aiming causing distractions. If you find difficulty, a 'blind' can be used which would prevent that eye from seeing anything even though it is kept open. Such blinds can be pieces of card which are attached to the rifle sight in such a way that it is in front of the non-aiming eye when viewing through the sights. If shooting spectacles are worn the blind can be like an opaque lens covering the non-aiming eye. These can usually be supplied with the spectacles. A typical system is shown in Fig 48.

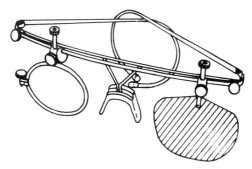

48 Shooting spectacles showing corrective lens and blind

A point which must be mentioned is the question of the 'master eye'. Most shooters have a 'master' or 'dominant' eye which is unconsciously over-used whenever the eyes are looking at something. It is usually the stronger eye and unless it is used as the sighting eye, there could be problems when trying to aim as it would disturb the concentration and distract the aim. To find out which is the dominant eye hold out the hands with the index fingers extended as in Fig 49. Keep both eyes open and line up the two fingers. Now close the left eye and see if the fingers are still aligned. If they are,

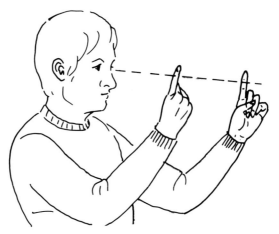

49 Finding the dominant eye. Line up index fingers with both eyes open. The master eye is the one for which the fingers remain aligned when the other is closed

then the right eye is the master eye and should be used as the aiming eye. If they are not aligned, try keeping the left eye open and close the right eye. If they now line up then it is the left eye which is the master eye. If neither line up and they are only aligned when both eyes are open then there is no preferential master eye and you can use whichever suits you. Usually, those who are left-handed also have a dominant left eye and vice versa for right-handers. If you are unlucky enough to be right-handed but have a dominant left eye or are left-handed and have a dominant right eye, you have problems. The solution is to purchase or make offset sight attachments so that when you are in the shooting position, the sights are aligned with the dominant eye.

### Sighting Equipment
The sighting equipment for a rifle consists of a foresight mounted near the muzzle and a rearsight mounted on the body. These must be accurately aligned and rigidly fixed to the barrel and body. The screws which hold the sight mounts onto the metalwork and the sights onto these mounts must be kept tight to avoid movement from shot to shot.

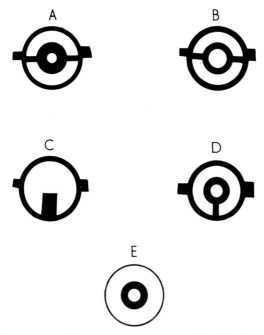

50 Sight elements: A, B, D – ring elements; C – blade (post) element; E – plastic element

FORESIGHT

The front sight consists of a tube fitted with removeable elements (Fig 25 on page 57). The elements come in a variety of shapes and sizes, the most popular of which is the ring element (Fig 50). Elements are usually made of metal and most rifles have a selection of the most common sizes and shapes. Of increasing popularity is the plastic element which is available in a variety of colours and has a chamfered hole in the centre; because of light refraction, it gives the impression of being a thin (or thick) black ring around the hole when viewed from the rearsight. The hole is easily enlarged if the shooter cannot find the correct size commercially. Another very useful foresight is the variable iris type (Fig 51) which can be changed in diameter merely by rotating the outer ring. With the variable foresight the hole diameter can be altered even in the middle of a match without fear of a change in the

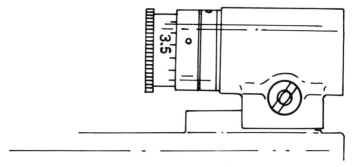

51 Variable iris foresight

point of impact of the pellet group. The size of the hole should be chosen so that a good contrast is seen between the black aiming market and the white target. Hole sizes for 10m shooting at UIT targets are usually chosen in the range 4.0mm−4.8mm diameter. Beginners should start off with a large size and then graduate to a smaller size as the hold becomes steadier.

Blade (post) foresight elements are also used but by a minority of shooters. The width of the blade should be chosen so that it appears to be the same width as the target aiming mark when sighting (Fig 52). The top of the blade should be aimed slightly below the aiming mark and the shooter should concentrate on maintaining a constant gap of white for each shot. The rearsight of course is adjusted so that with the selected point of aim the shot will hit the centre of the aiming mark. It is also important to ensure that the blade is upright even if you normally shoot with a cant. This can be done by filing off the location tangs on the element and rotating it in the foresight tube so that it is in the correct position when in the firing position.

Shooters with good eyesight sometimes find that they prefer the use of the blade foresight because they can judge the small gap of white in the 6 o'clock position better than the white annular gap when using a ring element. Variations in light level which can make the gap change, as found in out-door shooting, is not a problem with air rifle shooting

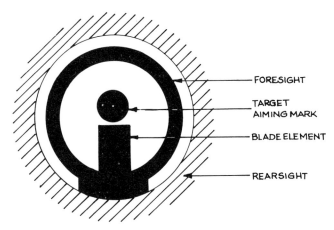

FORESIGHT

TARGET
AIMING MARK

BLADE ELEMENT

REARSIGHT

52 Sight picture using blade element

indoors. It should be used for a reasonable length of time to become accustomed to it properly before making a decision on whether it is any better than the ring.

THE REARSIGHT

Micrometer adjustment for elevation and windage are essential on target rifle rearsights. Rearsights supplied with the best air rifles are very accurate and generally very robust providing one takes reasonable care. They all have knobs which can adjust the sight in the order of $\frac{1}{6} - \frac{1}{8}$ minute of angle graduations. This gives something like 0.5mm displacement on the target at 10m. The sight adjustment should be checked regularly to ensure that no backlash is present. When the knob is rotated in either direction, it should move the sight an equal amount. If it does not, there is usually some adjustment available to take up backlash in the thread or it needs to be taken to someone who is able to repair sights. It is advisable to make a note of the sight adjustments for a particular range to be used as a datum. Datum for particular types of pellets should also be noted as there can be considerable changes in the point of impact of different pellet batches as well as different manufacturers. One can then make notes of different settings for different pellets and different ranges.

The size of the rear aperture is critical when trying to achieve a good sighting picture. Small variations in the diameter can cause large variations in definition when viewing the aiming mark against the white target. Most manufacturers only supply one or two interchangeable discs with different diameter holes but it is far better to purchase a variable rear aperture (iris) so that the best combination of rear and foresight apertures can be chosen for whatever lighting conditions you may be shooting under. Coloured filters can also be obtained, and with some adjustable rearsights a selection of filters is incorporated in the mechanism itself. Some shooters like using filters because it gives them better contrasts of the aiming mark and target.

In trying to obtain the optimum sight picture definition, the rearsight aperture adjustment is critical. What we are trying to obtain are sharp edges on the foresight aperture and on the aiming mark, with good contrast of the aiming mark, white target and foresight aperture. If you are unable to obtain sharp edges, it is preferable to try and obtain a clear foresight aperture than a clear aiming mark. A fuzzy aiming mark is preferable to a fuzzy foresight because it can be centred in a clear foresight whereas it is difficult to centre a clear aiming mark in a fuzzy foresight.

Cleanliness is essential in the sighting and all bits of dirt, hair, or fluff must be removed from the foresight and rearsight. It is amazing how many times a poor sight picture is caused by a very small piece of hair partially obstructing one of the sight apertures. A photographer's camel hair brush or puffer or a small aerosol is ideal for cleaning out the sights. Your shooting spectacles should also be cleaned before shooting. If everything has been cleaned and the optimum apertures chosen but a clear sight picture is still not seen, ensure that your eye is centred in the rearsight aperture as this too is a common error.

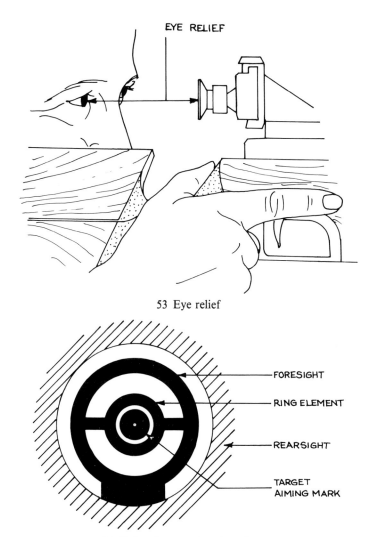

EYE RELIEF

53 Eye relief

FORESIGHT

RING ELEMENT

REARSIGHT

TARGET
AIMING MARK

54 Sight picture using ring element

## Eye Relief

This is the distance between the rearsight aperture and the aiming eye (Fig 53). It is not necessary to have the eye in contact with the rearsight; in fact, it can be detrimental as it might move the sight and any recoil could hurt and possibly cause flinching. There is no set distance for eye relief but it should be chosen so that it feels comfortable and a clear sight picture can be obtained without strain. Eye relief will also control the amount of background seen outside the foresight (Fig 54) and it is usually preferred to keep this to a minimum so that there are no distractions and head alignment is easier to achieve. Typical eye relief varies between 1–20cm.

## Positions and Firing the Shot

BASIC STANDING POSITION

Standing is the most difficult of all the shooting positions. A high degree of balance, extremely fine muscle control and a perfected firing technique is necessary to ensure that each shot is central and consistent. The only contact with the ground is through the feet and, as the centre of gravity of the body and rifle is high, the natural vibrations of the body caused by movement of the blood, heart and other bodily functions means that the shooter must use fine muscle control to maintain a steady position.

The shooter should take up a stance as shown in Fig 55. The feet are at 90 degrees to the target and about a shoulder width apart. Lean back slightly and twist to the left in order to achieve good balance, to impart some tension to the back muscles and to lock the spine. The centre of gravity of the body and rifle combined should then be between the feet, giving nearly equal weight on each foot (Fig 56). There is probably a tendency amongst most shooters to have slightly more weight on the front foot. The left elbow is positioned firmly on the hip or a little inside of the hip which would be thrust forward to support the elbow. The weapon weight by this means is supported by the bone structure of the forearm and left leg and not by muscular effort. If your elbow can't reach the hip, the rib cage will do the supporting.

The legs are kept straight and the knees flexible. The legs should not be stiffened but there will be a small amount of tension just sufficient to stabilise the position on aiming. The right knee may be slightly bent if it is felt to be advantageous

55 The standing position. Note the position of feet relative to direction of firing, back bend and elbow position on hip

56 The standing position. The weight of the rifle is supported by the bone structure and not through muscle power

in the position finally adopted.

The balance of the body is controlled by the head or, to be more precise, the balance mechanism contained in the ears. The balance mechanism is at its most efficient when the head is upright. Consequently when the rifle is held in the shoulder, the cheek-piece must be positioned so that the head is kept upright and not at an angle. The rifle may need to be canted to enable the head to remain upright but this is quite acceptable providing the cant is consistent from shot to shot.

The shoulders should be relaxed. Even the right shoulder should not have any noticeable tension in it although it is raised slightly higher than the other shoulder due to the hand having to grip the stock in order to give proper control to the trigger release. Tension in the right shoulder is the cause of many unexpected bad shots. This is because there is a tendency to tense the shoulder muscles and, as the muscles tire and cannot be kept with exactly the same amount of tension throughout the shoot, your co-ordination will be disturbed at the point of releasing the trigger, the effect of the recoil will change and hence the shot will be inaccurate. Develop the habit of follow through and you will see how the relaxation of various muscles which may have been in tension can cause the point of aim to alter even when using recoilless rifles.

The right hand holds the small of the stock (the 'pistol grip') securely. Some shooters hold the stock just firmly enough to support the hand and arm when squeezing the trigger but others grip it moderately hard and may pull the butt back harder into the shoulder. Each shooter will need to find his own optimum hold while bearing in mind that consistency must be maintained throughout the shoot. The right arm should be held with the minimum of tension in the muscles and can be held low in a relaxed position or held higher to give more shoulder contact.

The left arm supports the rifle by acting as a strut between the rifle and the body. The left arm and hand more than anything else determine how steady the rifle will be held. We discussed earlier how the arm was positioned, and from a study of Figs 57–64 it can be seen that there are many different methods of using the hand in the supporting role. The method used also determines the height of the rifle and the amount of back-bend which need be applied to have the

57 Hand position 1. This position should not be used because of the strain it produces in the fingers which would cause fatigue after a short time

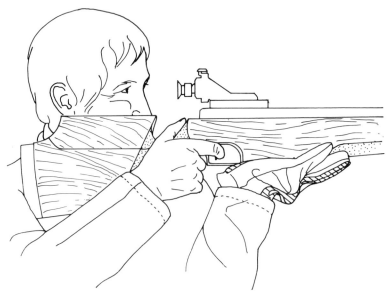

58 Hand position 2. This is a good position if you have long arms or a short upper torso. Not a common position

59 Hand position 3. A good position, the weight is taken through the hand and not the fingers

60 Hand position 4. A good position but there is some strain on the fingers

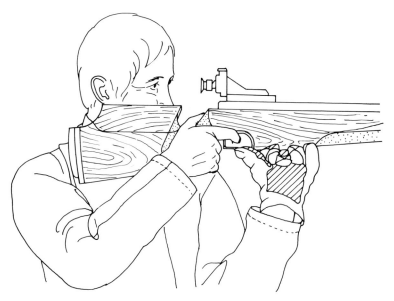

61 Hand position 5. The weight is taken through the fingers and thumb

62 Hand position 6. The 'V' position can be uncomfortable if the stock is too wide but it is not an uncommon position

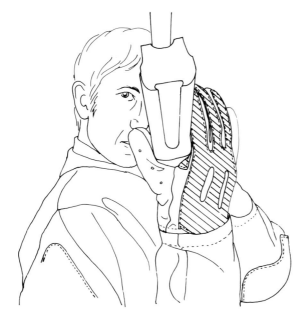

63 Hand position 7. This position has become popular but it does need the right limb proportions to use it without strain

64 Hand position 8. Commonly used because it gives a reasonably high rifle position without excessive back bend

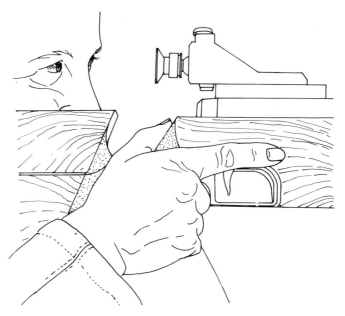

65 Safety position for trigger finger

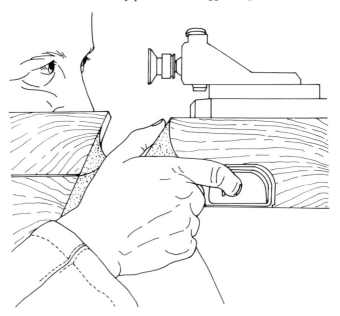

66 Ready position for trigger finger

17 A section of the main hall at Cardiff during the National Airweapon Championships

18 Granville Davies' Feinwerkbau 65, the grip modified with plastic wood to suit the individual hand

19 Left-handed Original 75 rifle, with the cheekpiece built up to suit individual neck length and shape of face

20 Prize-giving at the 1979 World Airweapon Championship in Seoul, South
Korea, when Britain took 3rd place

natural point of aim on the target. The position shown in Fig 57 is often used by beginners in their first efforts to support the rifle. This gives a high position without the need for excessive back-bend. Unfortunately, the muscles in the fingers and hand are being tensed and fatigue will follow fairly quickly, with resulting unsteadiness during a long shoot. As the muscles tire, the fingers will also slip on the stock with disastrous consequences. Only when the weight of the rifle is supported by the bone structure without the use of any muscles will the optimum steadiness be achieved and one should experiment with different hand positions along the lines shown in Figs 57–64 to find out which one gives you the steadiest position over the 2¼ hours time allowance to shoot the 60 shot match. All the muscles in the left arm and hand should be completely relaxed or just have a small amount of tension in order to achieve maximum steadiness of the rifle.

The trigger finger is normally located along the woodwork for safety reasons (Fig 65) while the position is being set up and finally the finger is placed on the trigger as the aim is centralised (Fig 66). It is important to ensure that the trigger finger does not touch the woodwork at this stage as the small movement of the finger could be transmitted to the rifle and the trigger release will not be smooth due to rubbing along the wood. Having ensured that the trigger finger is clear of the woodwork and correctly placed on the trigger, we must now be ready to apply pressure as the hold begins to settle. When the hold is steady or has the least movement and the sight picture appears correct, an increase in pressure on the trigger will fire the shot. This action should be automatic, smooth, and without jerking. The most sensitive part of the finger is the tip and this should be used to control the trigger. If the hold cannot be maintained whilst the trigger is released, then the shooter must remove pressure from the trigger, take a few breaths and then start the aiming cycle over again.

KNEELING POSITION

Although not internationally recognised for shooting air rifles, there are a number of competitions being held which expand air rifle shooting from the single position competition to a two position competition involving both the standing and kneeling positions. This will be welcomed by the small bore rifle shooters who already shoot in three positions (standing, kneeling, prone) as it will give them excellent training during the winter months for their summer outdoor programme. Air rifles are now available which are identical in shape, weight and balance to small bore 'standard' rifles hence affording the same feel when shooting with either rifle.

Some shooters find the kneeling position terribly difficult and uncomfortable but one has only to look at the high standards of shooting being achieved in small bore rifle shooting to realise that properly done, kneeling can be almost as steady as the prone position. Perhaps one day we will even see prone shooting with the air rifle being accepted but this is unlikely until the $CO_2$ gas systems become commonplace. This is because of the difficulty in cocking the rifle in the prone position using conventional spring systems.

To shoot in the kneeling position extra equipment is necessary. This equipment consists of a sling for the rifle and a kneeling roll to place under the ankle (Fig 67). The use of this equipment is seen in Fig 70. The sling is usually made of leather and is attached to the rifle near the front of the fore-end using the special channel on the underside of specialised target rifles. The other end of the sling is attached to the upper part of the left arm. The exact position is chosen to avoid the pulse present in the arm, otherwise there would be a movement transmitted to the rifle by this pulse beat which is not conducive to a good steady position. Do not be too dismayed if you find that your pulse beat is transmitted to the rifle as, with training, techniques will be evolved almost unconsciously which will reduce the problem. When in position, the sling should be adjusted so that it is tight enough to give support to the rifle and so avoid using muscles to keep

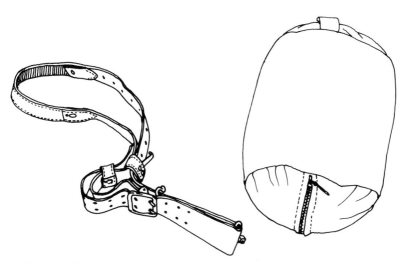

67 A sling for kneeling position usually made of leather, and a kneeling roll for support of right ankle.

the rifle sights aligned with the target.

The kneeling roll is a canvas or leather bag of up to 6in diameter when filled with sawdust, barley or other similar materials (Fig 67). When using the kneeling roll, the cushioning should give adequate firm support to the ankle. Foam rubber is not a good filling and should be avoided. The actual diameter can be less than 6in and depends on the size of boot, the support it gives and what feels comfortable.

Most experienced shooters use boots in the kneeling position. This is to give support to the ankle and to prevent the onset of 'pins and needles'. Nearly all beginners suffer from this within a few minutes of commencing to shoot but with training it becomes less of a problem and the top marksmen can stay in position for two hours or more without undue discomfort.

Additionally, the shooting jacket needs to be a little more sophisticated than for the standing position, as extra padding is needed for the left elbow and for the upper left arm (Fig 68). The elbow padding is to make the elbow more comfortable whilst resting on the knee, and the upper arm padding is

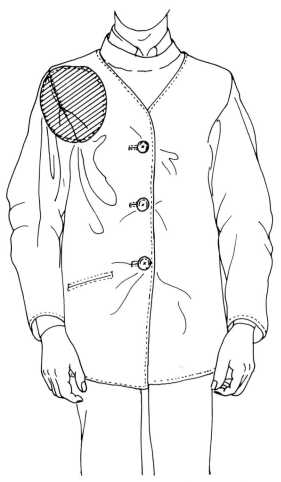

68 (and opposite) Shooting jacket showing style and padding. The size and shape of the jacket and padding are carefully controlled by rules

to relieve the pressure which is caused by the sling. All commercial shooting jackets are supplied complete with the necessary padding for all shooting positions but care must be taken to select only a shooting jacket which complies with UIT rules. If you make your own jacket, which many shooters do, make sure that the sizes, thicknesses and location of padding conforms to these rules. Many shooters

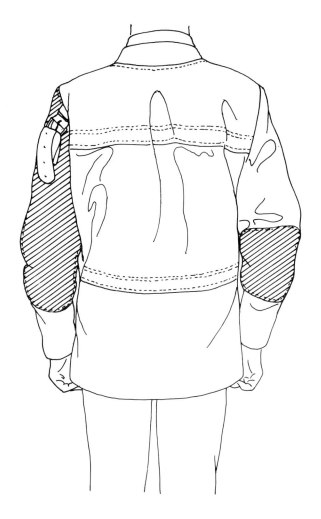

keep a special pair of trousers for kneeling. These should not
be tight as, if the thighs are being constrained, you may not
be able to sit on the right heel. Padding is allowed on the
knees and seat of the trousers (Fig 69). This makes kneeling
more comfortable and saves wear and tear on the trousers
which would otherwise wear out very rapidly at the knees.
Again, refer to the rules to make sure that the padding
complies.

The kneeling position is shown in Fig 70. The right foot is supported by the kneeling roll and is positioned centrally between the buttocks. The foot is vertical and very little pressure should be taken by the toes as the roll should do the supporting. The right knee is placed at a natural angle of 30–45 degrees to the line of fire. Because most of the weight is being taken by the ankle, very little weight is transmitted to the knee and it has more of a steadying influence than a supporting role. The left leg is placed almost in line with the line of sight. It may be 5–15 degrees off depending on the angle of the right leg. The left foot is placed naturally although this can be experimented with to see if turning it inwards slightly will reduce sideways wobble. The lower leg itself is placed so that it is vertical or near to the vertical.

The left elbow should be placed on top of the left knee so that the point of the elbow is situated in the little hollow of the knee. A certain amount of leeway is allowed here, and to be within the rules, the elbow can be anywhere within 10cm of the knee, forward or backward. When in the firing position, the left elbow and knee should be slightly to the left of the rifle rather than being directly underneath. The left hand supports the rifle and should be held in place by the sling so that there is no need to physically grip the rifle. The position of the hand should be chosen so that the hand feels comfortable and the forearm makes an angle of about 30 degrees to the horizontal. As mentioned earlier, the sling should give firm support so that the arm can be relaxed but the sights will still remain aligned to the target. The right arm is relaxed, apart from any small effort necessary to support the hand which will be grasping the pistol grip. No effort is used by the right arm and hand to guide the aim as it should be devoted to ensuring that a correct trigger release is achieved.

Vertical adjustment of the sight line is carried out by moving the butt so that when in a relaxed shooting position, the sights are aligned on the target. A small amount of vertical adjustment is available for the butt plate on the rifle

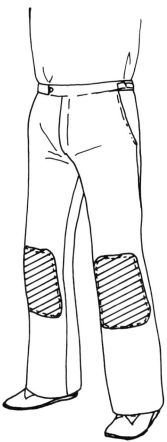

69 Shooting trousers, with pads on knees and seat (not shown)

so advantage should be taken of this to get maximum shoulder contact. Horizontal alignment is achieved by moving the whole body around using the left foot as a pivot. Trying to align the rifle by muscle movements will lead to erratic results and changes in the point of impact of the pellet, even though the sight picture and trigger let off were perfect. It is essential that every shot is fired with the rifle naturally aligned on the target so that a consistent point of impact will be achieved. This will avoid having to alter the sights to compensate for any muscle movement which would otherwise occur.

70 Upright kneeling position showing use of sling and kneeling roll

The two basic positions in kneeling are the upright (Fig 70) and forward positions (Fig 71). With the upright position, the spine is straight and upright and nearly the entire weight of the body is transmitted into the right ankle. The left leg only supports the weight of the rifle and a small part of the upper body weight. It is a very balanced position and can give a very steady hold, providing other factors like nervousness and, if

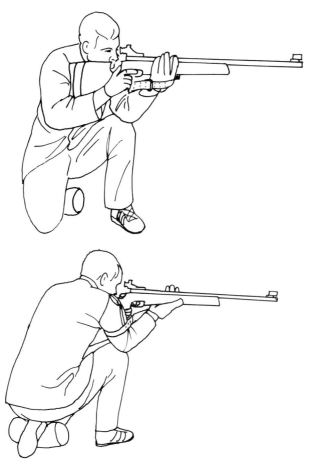

71 Forward kneeling position. Shows how more weight is positioned over left knee than in the upright position

shooting outdoors, wind are not present. The forward position is obtained by bending the back and consequently leaning forward, so that more weight is transmitted into the left leg. Not a lot of extra weight is transferred to the left leg but the act of slumping into the position, for that is what it is really, tends to throw weight forward and the centre of gravity moves towards the front foot. The exact weight distribution varies from person to person depending on body

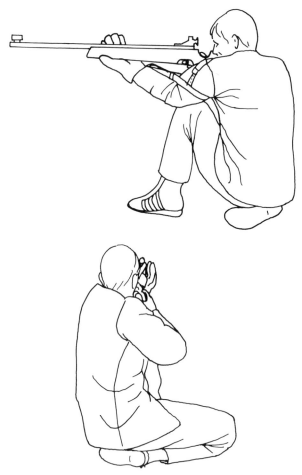

72 Low kneeling position. The lack of kneeling roll makes this an uncomfortable position for most shooters but has been used with success by prominent marksmen

structure and you will need to experiment to find the best position. In both positions, the head must be kept upright so that the ear balancing mechanism works at its most efficient. The eyes should also look straight out of the sockets and not through the eyebrows.

The shoulders are angled to the target and will vary

according to body formation and shooting position. There is a tendency for the shoulders to be angled more towards the target line of fire in the upright position and more at right angles in the forward position.

A third position which is sometimes used, but by a small minority of shooters is the low position (Fig 72). In this position a kneeling roll is not used and the shooter turns the right foot so that he sits on the inside of the foot and supports the body weight there. The left leg is thrown forward and is not usually upright like the other positions. Whether you adopt this position or not is dependent on the relative length of your body and limbs. Most shooters find this a difficult and uncomfortable position but if it suits you better then try it.

## Breathing

We must breathe to live but unfortunately, in shooting, breathing is a disadvantage as it moves the body and hence the rifle. We must minimise the effect of breathing by breath control. When getting into position breathing can be normal and uncontrolled. In the final settlement of the position the breathing must come under control and becomes shallower with the emphasis being made on breathing out as it is in the breathing out stage that concentration must start the process of eliminating all movement of the rifle. Final elimination of movement is when the target is centralised in the sight and breathing is stopped for the few seconds needed to fire the shot. The breath should not be held for more than up to, say, 8 seconds as the lack of oxygen will cause loss of concentration and an overwhelming desire to take a breath. There is also a danger that if the breath is held too long, the shooter will hurriedly try to get the shot away before having to take a breath and in nearly every case will regret the action because the shot is bad. If you feel you are running out of breath, stop the firing process and take a few deep breaths or even come off the aim altogether and start afresh. The breathing pause includes the 'follow through' action (see below) as well as the final aiming and trigger let-off, hence a hurried shot may result in a breath being taken before the follow through is completed.

The action of breathing out is a relaxing one and it can be put to more use in quelling the nerves or 'butterflies' that are experienced in match shooting. More on this is said in Chapter 9.

**Follow Through**

Follow through is the act of maintaining the hold and concentration after the trigger has been squeezed until the pellet has left the barrel. Follow through is more important in air rifle shooting than in small bore or full bore shooting because the pellet is slower than a bullet in clearing the barrel and so more time needs to be allowed for follow through. One other aspect of follow through which is little realised is that it prevents the relaxation of any muscles which were being used to hold the rifle steady, after trigger release. The relaxation of these muscles can start immediately the trigger is activated and before the pellet is out of the barrel. This will cause unexplained wild shots so the shooter must develop the discipline of firing the shot and then maintain the aim until any movement due to firing the shot has stopped. This is easy to do for recoil-type rifles but is more difficult to gauge for recoilless rifles as there may be no rifle movement. However, the act of maintaining the aim after squeezing the trigger will mean that sufficient time will have elapsed for the pellet to clear the barrel. With beginners it is better to err on too long a follow through than too short. The expert shot with a fast rhythm will appear to have no follow through but in fact he does maintain his hold for the minimum of time necessary, much to the confusion of some spectators.

**Grouping**

When practising and when sighting-in prior to commencing a match it is important to ensure that your group is centralised. The group we are discussing is a number of shots fired at a

73 A typical group showing a 'flyer' which must be ignored when deciding on the position of the centre of the group

single diagram where we estimate the centre of the group and its distance from the centre of the target. Fig 76 shows a typical group which could be fired by a shooter depending on his ability. From our shots we must try and eliminate those shots we know are a mistake and concentrate on those which were as good as we could make them. Having decided on the centre of the group, the shooter must then estimate how far it is from the centre of the target and move the sight controls to centre the group over the target centre. On most match quality rifles the rearsights (Fig 24 on page 56) have what is called click adjustment. A study of the rifle handbook will give you how much the 'click' will move the shot on the target at 10m. It is usually around 0.5mm per click which adds up to approximately 5 clicks to move the point of impact of the pellet from one scoring ring to the next. So if the shooter estimates the centre of the group to be on the seven ring at 12 o'clock, it will take 15 clicks to centre it on the bull (Fig 74). If you also cant the rifle, it will be necessary to give windage adjustment to the left of several clicks depending on the amount of cant used.

Whenever possible, shoot for groups before starting a match and, whilst in training sessions, concentrate on groups to try and reduce their size, as well as to correct the sights. One can start out a training session by firing 5 shot groups

74 Off-set group. This group gives clear indication of the need for an elevation adjustment of the sights

75 A typical group reduction exercise commencing with trying to get all five shots within the '6' ring

76 A smaller group with all five shots within the '8' ring

and saying to oneself, 'I must get all 5 shots within the "6" ring', and carry on until this is achieved (Fig 75). It is beneficial to start all training sessions with a goal and reduction of groups is an ideal goal. Having achieved all 5 shots within the 6 ring one can either try and get 10 shots within that area or reduce the area by trying to place all 5 shots withing the 8 ring (Fig 73). Even the experts carry out group reduction exercises, but their aim will be to score nothing less than a 9 with 10 shots and then nothing less than a 10 with 5 shots.

# 7 Target Pistol Shooting

**The Sighting System**

Eyesight and eye correction is a critical factor in pistol shooting and the general principles described in the previous Chapter should be followed.

For target shooting the foresight used should be a parallel post with square edges and flat top as shown in Fig. 77. The width of the post should be chosen so that it appears equal to the width of the aiming mark. The rearsight should be broad and flat with a notch which gives adequate clearance around the foresight to enable the shooter to easily see when the foresight is not in the centre of the rearsight. If the notch is too narrow it will be difficult to centralise the foresight because bending of the light will occur which would make the gap seem wider than it really is, and less easy to see that an equal strip of light is visible on the right and left of the foresight. As a guide to the width of the notch, the gap on each side of the foresight should equal about half the apparent diameter of the aiming mark (see Fig 78).

77 Parallel post foresight

When aiming at the target, the top of the foresight should be held below the aiming mark with a gap of white which is large enough to avoid errors in gauging the thickness of white due to light distortion. This generally indicates that a gap of about two scoring rings is needed (see Fig 79). This method is preferable to trying to aim for the bull by holding the foresight in the centre of the black, as it is very difficult to gauge when the black foresight is in the centre of the black aiming mark.

Target pistols are usually equipped with a rearsight on which adjustments can be made for vertical and horizontal errors (Fig 27 on page 59). Always sight in the pistol for the

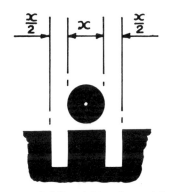

78 Recommended foresight and rearsight widths

79 Gap between foresight and aiming mark should be the width of two rings or optical illusion may occur

particular range and lighting conditions. Adjustments for vertical and horizontal errors must be done using the rearsight and never by moving your point of aim. Once the brain has become trained to accept a certain sight picture one should not try to alter it by moving the point of aim. If the sight has click adjustment and/or a scale, find out and memorise how much each click or graduation on the scale moves the point of impact on the target. Many points have been lost even by experts in being unsure how to move the sights if the point of impact appears to have changed during the shoot. Don't make that mistake!

## The Stance

The basic position for pistol shooting is just as important as for rifle shooting. Many of the shooting techniques are the same. Balance, control of muscles and a perfected firing technique are all important. The only contact with the ground is through the feet and the natural body movements must be controlled by fine adjustments of muscle tension in order to minimise their effect on steadiness of aim. The pistol shooter has less support for the pistol than the rifle shooter for his weapon, as no support is allowed for the arm holding the pistol. A typical position is shown in Fig 80. However, to be fair, the target, although situated at the same range, does have larger scoring rings. In fact the degree of difficulty of the rifle and pistol targets appears to be the same for the top shooters as the winning scores are similar.

The pistol shooter takes up his stance so that when he raises his arm to aim his natural point of aim should be at the target. The feet should be at approximately 45–90 degrees to the line of sight to the target, but the general position should be chosen so that the optimum state of balance is achieved with the pistol raised and aiming at the target. The weight will be equally distributed on the feet. The pistol arm must be held straight and the arm and upper part of the body should be held rigidly. If the natural point of aim on the target is not achieved, sideways movement will need to be carried out by moving the feet, *not* twisting the body. Vertical adjustment, however, is usually taken care of by bending from the waist. Having taken up position, it can be enlightening to aim at the target, then lower the pistol, close the eyes, raise the pistol to

80 Pistol shooting stance. Note relaxed stance and position of feet relative to direction of firing

the target and open the eyes again. It is surprising how far off the target you can be when doing this test and adjustments must be made to one's position until this test results in the aim being on the target.

The legs should be straight and the knees flexible with just sufficient tension to stabilise the position. Any shoes or boots worn should not have too soft a sole. A soft, spongy sole will prevent the shooter achieving good balance as he will be constantly adjusting the muscle tension in his legs and feet to overcome excessive movement arising from the spongy sole.

A flat firm sole of the type used by rifle shooters is much more preferable. A stiff boot is not necessary as it is the fine movement in position we are trying to eliminate, not the excessive movement, which is all that strong boots might reduce.

The head should be upright and turned towards the target without straining the neck muscles. The pistol when raised should have the sights in line with the eyes without having to bend the head.

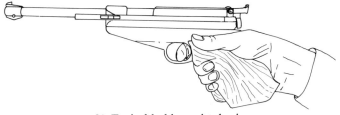

81 Typical hold on pistol grip

To achieve the steadiest, most consistent aim it is important to grip the pistol correctly (Fig 81). The grips provided with the pistol are rarely ideal and some customising is usually necessary. Strict limits are enforced when taking part in competitions run under UIT rules with respect to dimensions and the customised pistol must fit within a box measuring 420 × 200 × 50mm. Because of the need to compress the spring or air a good grip is necessary and it should make as much contact with the hand as possible so that when in position there is only one hand grip which feels right. With a correctly shaped stock, the centre line of the barrel should intersect with the natural 'V' of the hand as

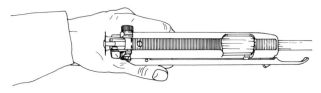

82 Holding the pistol showing intersection with the natural 'V' of the hand

shown in Fig 82. If the shooter is a handy woodworker he can probably make his own grips but if not then it would be advisable to go to someone who specialises in providing custom built grips. Those unable to make the grips or find anyone who could do it for them, could try using plastic wood or other types of compound to build up the sections of the grip to fit the hand (Fig 11). The centre of gravity of the pistol should be in the region of the trigger. Much of the weight would then be bearing down on the three fingers underneath the trigger guard which should be holding the pistol firmly against the ball of the thumb. The underside of the trigger guard will be against the middle finger which gives a good hand grip location as well as transferring the weight of the pistol into the hand. The thumb should not apply any pressure but should rest lightly on the thumb rest or against the side of the pistol. The forefinger should be clear of the pistol except where it rests on the trigger. Under no circumstances should the forefinger be supported by the trigger guard as this will artificially appear to increase the trigger weight and also cause an inconsistent finger movement on the trigger.

The left hand is usually an embarrassment as it has no useful task to do. All that one can do is to put it somewhere where it doesn't get in the way and where it can be completely forgotten about. The usual places are in your pocket, behind the back, in your waistband or even just hanging loose by your side.

**Aiming and Trigger Release**
Aiming and trigger release is one of the most important lessons to be learned by the beginner. Even the more experienced shooter has difficulties on occasion with these tasks. We shall discuss each one separately and then how to combine them into the integrated act of shooting.

A common mistake in aiming is to focus the eye on the target rather than on the sights. By aiming this way small errors in sight alignment cannot be seen and wild shots will appear on the target. It is impossible to focus on both the sights and the target so the shooter's focus and concentration should be on the alignment of the sights. If the shooter finds he cannot focus clearly on the sights, then a visit to the optician to obtain corrective spectacles would help their shooting enormously. Whether to keep both eyes open or to close one is a question often asked. In general it is less tiring to keep both open. However, some shooters find that they cannot focus correctly on the sights as the dominant eye, which should be used for sighting, sometimes gives away to the less dominant eye. If this does occur the wearing of a blind to cover the non-aiming eye will be necessary.

In pistol shooting it is almost impossible to hold the pistol still when aiming at the target. There is always a small amount of wobble even with the experts. However, as the pistol can group well inside the 10 ring, a small amount of error can be tolerated and yet still hit the 10 ring. Consequently the shooter must learn to accept that a perfect hold is rarely achievable and that a degree of wobble will be present. This will leave his mind free to concentrate on perfect alignment of the foresight and rearsight.

Trigger release should be an automatic reflex action when the aim is aligned correctly. To achieve this, the trigger technique must be perfected so that as the sights and aiming mark are lined up the trigger release is completed. This may sound very difficult to a beginner as he is probably having considerable trouble keeping the sights aligned because of unsteadiness. However, even when there is a lot of wobble, an automatic trigger release as the sights do line up will give much better results than trying to line up the sights first and then trying to go through the action of trigger release. This is because the shooter's concentration will have moved from sight alignment and holding the pistol steady, to trying to squeeze the trigger. There is thus an inherent delay between the message from the brain saying that the sights are aligned and the muscles activating the trigger. The result will be wild, inconsistent shots.

The better technique is to carry out the final aiming and trigger release together so that the shooter is surprised when the shot is fired. To do this, the aiming process is started, and when the wobbles become smaller, the finger gradually squeezes the trigger until without warning the shot breaks and, with training, this should be when the sights are perfectly aligned. This should all happen in a time span of 5-8 seconds from the commencement of the final aim. If it takes longer than this, it would be better to come down off aim and after a pause recommence the aiming process again.

Whenever a shooter picks up the pistol and aims at the target, it can be noticed that the initial aim is unsteady; then comes a period of relative steadiness and then again a period of unsteadiness. It is during that short period of relative steadiness that the shot must be fired. If the shot is not fired in that period, come down off aim or take a few deep breaths and then have another go. The integrated act of aiming and firing must be practised constantly until it is automatic and occurs without thinking about carrying out the separate actions.

## Follow Through

After firing the shot, the temptation to put the pistol down and look through the spotting telescope or return the target must be resisted for a short period to allow the pellet to leave the barrel. This is called the follow through period and the shooter should continue his aim and hold for several seconds after trigger release. If this is not done, unexpectedly wild shots will appear on the target even though the aim was good at trigger release. There is also the possibility that the brain will anticipate the moment of trigger release and start the premature relaxation of the muscles holding the pistol and the pistol will move as the pellet is moving down the barrel. The knowledge that follow through will be carried out means that the brain will not anticipate relaxing the muscles until after the pellet has left the barrel. The shooter should also try to calculate the probable position of the shot and then check to see if they were right by looking at the target through the telescope or when it is returned. Even with the so-called recoilless pistols, it is enlightening to note whether any recoil or jump occurs and whether the pistol moves due to involuntary muscle action or, of course, a bad trigger let-off.

## Fault Correction

The average club shooter does not normally have the benefit of good coaches and fault correction will depend on critical self-analysis. Grouping is usually the most informative means of fault diagnosis. To do this, fire 10 shots at the target whilst trying to maintain the same aiming area and grip on the pistol. Don't forget the follow through and avoid looking at the shot position on the target between shots. Typical groups and diagnoses are shown in Figs 83–9.

Reduction of group sizes is an excellent training exercise and the system used for rifle shooting is equally applicable to pistol shooting (see Chapter 6).

83 Snatching the trigger or not concentrating on sight alignment

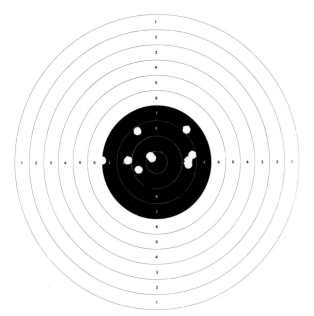

84 Incorrect stance causing horizontal movements of body

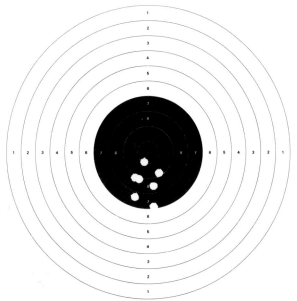

85 Lack of concentration causing foresight to drop relative to rearsight, or not maintaining gap between foresight and aiming mark

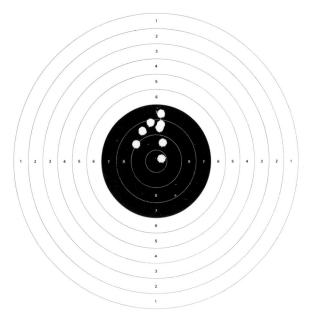

86 Lack of concentration causing foresight to be higher than rearsight, or allowing gap between foresight and aiming mark to close resulting in light distortion

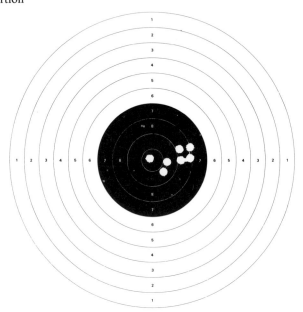

87 Allowing sights to drift to the right relative to aiming mark

88 Good group but sights need elevation adjustment to bring group down into centre

89 Good group but sights need horizontal adjustment

# 8 Running Boar Target Shooting

**Introduction**

Running boar target air rifle shooting is the newest addition to the air rifle scene. It is now recognised as an International event and is included in European and World Shooting Championships. The competition is based on the 50m small-bore rifle event but scaled down for shooting at 10m.

The target consists of a picture of a wild boar with circular scoring rings located just behind the shoulders (Fig 90). The scoring rings are identical in diameter to the normal 10m air rifle target but the '10' on the Boar Target is a '9' on the static target so all the rings are one point less and of course are hard to hit because this target moves! It is held in a carriage which moves across a 2m gap before disappearing from sight. The speed with which it covers the gap is variable according to the competition. There are two types of competition: one consisting of 20 shots at a fast run target and 20 shots at a slow run target, and the other being 20 shots + 20 shots at mixed run targets.

In the slow run the target appears from behind cover and crosses the 2m gap in 5 seconds before disappearing behind cover. During this time a single shot is fired at the target. After a short time to allow reloading of the rifle, the target appears running in the opposite direction across the space and is fired at. This process carries on until 20 shots have been fired plus the 2 sighting shots (one in each direction) fired at the commencement of the runs. After a period of time whilst other shooters have their turn at the slow runs, you then return to the firing point for the fast runs. The target crosses the 2m gap in 2½ seconds during which time

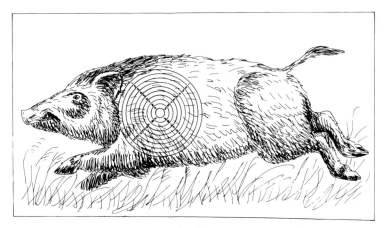
90 Running boar target

you must fire the shot. Two shots are allowed as sighters and the 20 shots at the fast run then take place. The time between shots in both the slow and fast runs is about 12-16 seconds.

The second competition is the mixed run event. This consists of a total of 4 sighting shots and 40 shots fired at the crossing target but the speed of the run is chosen so that we have a mixture of slow and fast runs. The mixture of runs is not completely random but must conform to certain rules and there must be 20 slow runs and 20 fast runs with an equal number from each side. The runs are chosen so that the shooter is unable to predict whether the next run is fast or slow and there must not be more than 5 continuous runs at the same speed.

**Technique**
When taking your place on the firing point, the feet are positioned so that the legs are at 45−90 degrees to the target, and nothing is to touch the table or wall. Whilst preparing for the target to appear, the rifle must be held so that the butt is below the waist and touching the hip or abdomen. As the target appears the rifle is brought up to the shoulder and the aim taken (Fig 91). It is important that you are mentally prepared so that the appearance of the target is not a surprise

91 Taking aim running boar target. Note the upright head position

and you easily pick up the appropriate aim whilst tracking it. The sight cross hairs or post is sighted on the appropriate aiming point chosen and the rifle follows the movement of the target until a satisfactory aim is achieved and the shot is fired. The turning motion of the body should be smooth, not jerky, as the sight must follow the aiming mark without stopping for it to catch up, or accelerating the movement to catch up with the aiming mark. It is a mistake to try to follow the target by just swinging the arms, and for the beginner might show only short-term advantages before performance would be limited by an incorrect style. Even after firing the shot, the rifle must continue to follow through, otherwise the shots will not be consistently placed on the target due to the movement of the target which takes place whilst the shot is moving up the barrel and through the air. Following through ensures that the pellet has time to leave the barrel whilst the target is still being followed and gives the pellet a sideways velocity following the target.

The left hand supports the rifle well forward of the fore-end beyond the point of balance. The fore-end should be shaped so that a good position or hold can be obtained and the swing of the rifle as it follows the target can be controlled easily and consistently. On the Feinwerkbau and Walther running boar rifles, the fore-end has been specially shaped and roughened so that a good non-slip position can be obtained, and its length extended beyond that of the normal rifle so that the hand can hold the rifle well forward. The left arm must not rest on the hip or chest and a sling is not allowed.

The butt plate can be curved or straight. The curved type was popular when running boar shooting was introduced because it was thought that it would help locate the butt in the shoulder, but ideas have changed and there is a growing preference for a straight butt plate. Again it is a matter of personal preference. The butt length should be chosen so that it can be held firmly in the shoulder without slipping.

**Sighting**

Telescopic sights are used because of the necessity to select accurately the aiming point and this cannot easily be done without such sights. Beginners can use relatively primitive telescopic sights to start with, and progress to better sights if the sport is sufficiently appealing for them to spend the money on more sophisticated equipment. A 4–6× power telescope is sufficient for many shooters, although the more expert may progress to powers in the region of 12×.

The point of aim on the target can be any easily defined mark such as the nose or the eye. Sometimes an area of aim such as the jowl or between the nose and the eye is used. The scoring rings themselves are not chosen as an aiming point because of the poor definition of the rings.

The graticules used can be cross hairs, dots or adjustable twin posts. Multiple dots and twin posts are specialist telescopic sights and are expensive, so many shooters only use a cross hair or single post. If you can choose between post or cross hairs, it is preferable to go for the cross hair as there is less obstruction of target detail than when using a post. Multiple dots and twin posts are used because the same aiming point may be chosen for both runs by using one post for one direction and the other for the reverse runs.

With multiple dots, three dots are used as graticules which are fixed and cannot be altered. There is the central dot which can be used for zeroing of the sight against a static target and displaced on each side of the central dot, there is a further dot which can be used to give the appropriate lead, depending on the direction of travel of the target.

Twin posts are adjustable so that the shooter can select his favourite aiming mark and alter the position of the post to line up on that mark. The two posts are necessary to give the lead in both target directions. The other advantage with twin posts is that they can be adjusted initially for the slow runs and then further adjusted for the fast runs so that the same aiming mark can be used. Because of this facility, one has to bear a significant price increase over a fixed graticule sight but they are probably essential for top shooters in order to compete on level terms with each other.

Care must be taken when mounting the telescope to ensure that it is sufficiently above the loading chamber to allow easy insertion of the pellet. This may mean a slightly higher sightline to barrel line than usually associated with using a 'scope' sight, and it may be necessary to increase the height of the cheek-piece, so that when the butt is brought to the shoulder, the cheek-piece is in contact with your cheek. This should give adequate support and location so that you can see through the sights without having to move your head. The head is usually held upright although a slight forward tilt is sometimes used. Some rifles are fitted with adjustable cheek-pieces but where no adjustment is provided, the cheek-piece can be built up using pieces of target, wood, leather and masking tape until it fits your face and you are in line with the sight. If you do not make the rifle fit you, valuable seconds will be lost whilst you are trying to get your head in the correct position in relation to the sight while the target is moving, leaving very little time to fire an accurate shot. Do not forget to adjust the position of the 'scope to give the correct eye relief so that the sight picture fills the whole of the

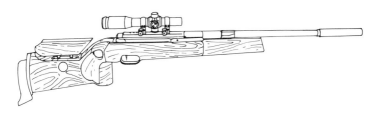

92 Running boar rifle showing thumb-hole stock

eyepiece. Also the focusing must be adjusted to have a clear target and reticule with no parallax effects. Many scopes available do not focus down to 10m so always make sure when buying one that it can focus down to the correct range.

## Equipment

The rifles available range from the inexpensive to the expensive recoilless type such as the Walther and Feinwerkbau. Naturally, as when shooting at static targets, there are limits to the performance which can be achieved with cheaper rifles and telescopes but these are ideal for the beginner. If you already possess a recoilless rifle for shooting at the 10m and 6yd static targets, then these may be suitable for running boar when fitted with a telescopic sight. It is also possible to use thumb-hole stocks (Fig 92) under the running boar rules. A thumb-hole stock may help you to raise the rifle to the shoulder and to grip it more firmly and consistently but their use is a matter of personal preference.

Clothing should be less restrictive than in static air rifle shooting as you must have freedom to move easily. The jacket should not be tight or of a stiff material but should allow easy arm and body movement. The only padding needed is a shoulder pad of non-slip material so that the butt does not slip when it is brought into position. A soft glove may be used on the left hand if required but not the padded type used in static target shooting. Boots are not essential as they do not need to give support to the ankles, but they can be worn if required for personal comfort. A flat sole to the boot or shoe can give better, more consistent floor contact. Training shoes are often used but should not be the type often used by joggers which have thick spongy soles.

A shooting hat can be worn and may prevent reflections in the eyepiece of the telescopic sight but care should be taken to ensure that it does not cause an obstruction when raising the rifle into the aiming position. Ear defenders or ear plugs can be worn to aid concentration by reducing background noise levels, but again, choose carefully so that they do not become a nuisance when the cheek is held against the cheek-piece. They are not really necessary to protect your hearing as the noise levels are not high when using an air rifle.

**Scoring System**

As you do not retrieve the target after each shot, a system of indicating the value and position of the shot on the target has been developed. This is an indicator operated by the marker located on the target apparatus consisting of a sort of clock face where the value of the shot is indicated by the red clock hand, and the position of the shot is indicated using the clock method − shot value 9 at 10 o'clock. If you fire the shot early enough, you will be able to see it in the sight before it disappears behind the screen but usually the shot is fired just before reaching the screen, so it disappears before you can note the shot value and position. On more sophisticated systems and at international matches, a video camera and monitor is used so that the shooter can see his target and the position of his shot after each run. This also adds spectator value to the sport as it can be seen from behind the firing point.

Even if you are not very competitive, a lot of fun can be had shooting running boar targets as it is very much like sporting shooting and may satisfy your hunting instinct whilst not killing off the wildlife which we would all like to retain for future generations.

# 9 Physical and Mental Training

Physical fitness is important if you are determined to become a champion. In order to shoot well the muscles must be in good shape and toned to an adequate degree so that the course of fire can be complete without fatigue affecting performance. How can one become fatigued just shooting, you may ask. Well, a little thought can easily show how it happens.

The men's international course of fire for air rifle and air pistol shooting is 2¼ hours. The weapon is picked up for 60 shots and perhaps up to 15 sighters, if the shot is fired at the first attempt. However, several attempts for some shots are likely particularly if the shooter has problems. Assuming an average of 1½ attempts per shot and using an 11lb weight rifle then the competitor will have picked up 75 × 11 × 1½ = 1237.5lb. In other words, over half a ton will have been lifted during the competition; the rifle is then held while striving to relax the muscles and yet retain that fine control over body and mind to stop all movement whilst the trigger is squeezed. The shooter must also try to concentrate exclusively on each shot for the best part of 2¼ hours. The mental fatigue is probably more noticeable than physical fatigue, but they do go hand in hand and, if we can become physically fit, the benefit of our fitness will show in greater mental endurance.

**General Fitness**
General fitness can be achieved by following a course of physical instruction in locally organised keep fit courses, at evening classes or at your club (if you're lucky to belong to

such a well-organised club). Alternatively, you can follow the 5BX plan (*Physical Fitness*, Penguin) produced by the Royal Canadian Air Force which is an ideal plan for shooters to follow. The Aerobics method (*The New Aerobics* by Kenneth Cooper) is another good system, particularly for the cardio-respiratory system (heart, lungs, blood vessels).

The 5BX programme has been designed to enable any healthy man to achieve physical fitness by devoting eleven minutes a day to carrying out a balanced set of exercises. The plan consists of six charts arranged in progression. Each chart has given exercises to be carried out in the same order and in a set time limit. These exercises are carried out regularly and progression is made from chart to chart as each one gradually demands more effort. One does not necessarily complete all six charts as they are also graduated for age, and a man aged 45 years plus would stop at chart 2 whilst an 18-25 year old would progress half way up chart 5.

Aerobics refers to a variety of exercises that stimulate the heart and lungs for a period of time sufficiently long to produce beneficial changes in the body. Most physical sports that increase heart rate and lung activity can give a certain amount of benefit and can be classed as a form of aerobics but only if they are carried out for a sufficient period of time. Typical aerobics exercises are running, swimming, cycling and jogging. Squash, tennis, basketball, skiing and skating are others. They all have one thing in common and that is that they make you work and cause an increase in demand for oxygen.

An aerobics exercise programme is designed to increase the maximum amount of oxygen that the body can process in a given time. The results of this exercise is to produce a more powerful heart, more efficient lungs and a good vascular system. The exercises carried out must raise the heart rate for a sufficient duration; all exercises will differ in their ability to meet this criterion as can be realised if one compares running with squash. In order to get the same benefits from these two exercises one must maintain a running programme of 1½ miles in 12-15 minutes carried out 5 times a week compared to squash where the game must last 40 minutes and be carried out 5 times per week. A sport like golf would need a great deal longer than this and need to be carried out just as frequently. Hence, if time is short, it would be better to do running as an aerobic exercise rather than any other. It is also probably the cheapest form of exercise!

*The New Aerobics* by Kenneth Cooper contains a number of training plans for men and women of all ages. The plans are all based on a points system so that one can choose from a number of different exercises, the frequency and duration of each giving a satisfactory level of fitness. If you do different sports from those in the plans, similar points allocations are given so that one can carry out a number of different exercises and sports to give the required number of points to maintain fitness.

The strength and endurance of the body is improved by carrying out a system of exercise, and research has shown that the heart of a fit person has a less rapid acceleration of pulse rate under stress and returns more rapidly to normal after stress than that of an unfit person. Exercise also tends to reduce the pulse rate below that which was normal before the programme of exercise was carried out. All of these benefits help the shooter to give a peak performance under the conditions of stress that occur in matches. The sense of well-being is also a benefit that cannot be overlooked as it can give the fit shooter a psychological boost to know that he is more physically prepared for the match than the majority of the other competitors.

Dynamic games such as squash, badminton, tennis, football, table tennis also improve general fitness, and give the shooter a change from his shooting training. In deciding to carry out any form of exercise programme it is advisable to have a medical check up, particularly if you are over the age of thirty. All exercises should be developed gradually to prevent strained muscles and ligaments and to prevent over-straining the heart.

**Special Fitness**

To hold the body and rifle or pistol perfectly still whilst the aim is taken and the shot fired, demands that certain groups of muscles be developed in addition to those used in general fitness training.

The best way to train these groups of muscles is to carry out dry firing exercises. Dry firing is performed in the same way as live firing except that the weapon is not cocked and no pellet is used. It can be carried out in the comfort of your own home by making up a target with a black circle representative of the aiming mark when viewed through the sights and at the same height as that on the firing range. The training is performed by putting on the appropriate shooting attire and getting into position as if to fire the weapon. The shooter then goes through the normal procedure of aiming, stopping all movement, squeezing the trigger and following through as though the shot had been fired.

Alternatively, practise holding the weapon in position for extended periods of time to accustom the muscles to a sustained hold. Some shooters can dry fire for long periods without becoming bored, but if you do become bored try doing it for shorter periods but more of them.

During dry firing imagine that the shot is going to be a live one and take the utmost care to hold the rifle still on the target for a long enough period to release the shot. Live firing mixed up with dry firing is another stage which checks to ensure that muscle control is consistent and the result can be seen on the target, reinforcing ones prediction of where the shot should land or showing a fault in technique.

The training and strengthening of muscles is a slow process and results are not seen quickly. Fitness training gives a general improvement in blood circulation, lungs and muscle tone which will ensure that the physical aspects of shooting do not hold back the progress of the marksman. The general fitness training should be completed 4-6 weeks before the match season begins in earnest. Special fitness training is carried out continually, even through the match season.

## Mental Training

The beginner devotes most of his efforts to achieving a good, stable stance, a good aim and trigger release. As his hold develops and he takes part in various competitions, he begins to realise that there is something more to shooting than just these aspects, as his match scores are usually not so good as his training scores. What is preventing good match scores is match pressure. In recent years, more research has gone into ways of overcoming this than in the shooting position itself and, if you are to succeed, it will be necessary to follow a programme of mental training. Mental training should contain work on concentration, mental discipline, match pressure and relaxation.

CONCENTRATION

Full concentration for every shot fired is essential if a good performance is to be obtained. A good position will be degraded without absolute concentration on each shot.

Concentration on body control is a prime objective. If the body can be stilled on the aim, then trigger release should be automatic on seeing the optimum sight picture. Physical fitness helps to tone the muscles so that they are efficient and do not fatigue, but it is mental concentration that is used to stop all body movement for the duration of the aim and trigger release. The mechanics of shooting – position, sighting, trigger release – are relatively easily learnt, but the development of concentration is much more difficult and is often the reason why quite a number of shooters, who have a good position, are fit, have good eyesight and practice regularly, cannot achieve their goal of being a champion because of inconsistency during the match. It only needs a momentary lapse in concentration to produce a wide shot which completely spoils a run of good shots. Concentration must be 100 per cent on each of the shots being fired in the match.

What does the shooter concentrate on whilst shooting? There is no simple answer to this as it has been noted that when a shooter is performing well, he is not concentrating on a particular group of muscles but has a general awareness of the muscles being used to steady the body. A rhythm develops as body control, aim and trigger release peak together and almost without thinking the shot is a good one.

At other times he is aware of having to concentrate on particular sets of muscles, those which he feels are the cause of unsteadiness, and then perhaps concentration moves from muscles to aiming or to trigger release. In general it appears that concentration should be on eliminating any outside thoughts and letting the body find its natural balance and stillness, concentrate on the sight picture and let the subconscious do all that is necessary to still the body to achieve the optimum aim. The subconscious will also be responsible for achieving the correct trigger release at the instant that the mind realises that all the elements to produce a good shot are together.

All thought should be positive. One should think of how good it is to be shooting rather than what you could be doing at home or at work. Don't think about bad shots or you will repeat them. Think about the good shots, visualise them and more good shots will be produced.

If your thoughts start wandering off the firing of the shot, try concentrating on a particular group of muscles – arm, shoulder, neck; even if you do not consider them as problem areas, it will keep your mind concentrating.

Maximum performance occurs when you have eliminated all thought about how well you're doing and are focusing concentration on your objective. Your objective in shooting is to eliminate all body movement whilst obtaining a satisfactory (perfect) aim and an unconscious trigger release. Focusing is the essence of concentration, in which you are using all your senses to make small adjustments in muscle control to eliminate all body movement and mental activity. It is possible to think too much on performance but never to focus too sharply.

RELAXATION

Mental tension produced by match pressure results in muscle tension which can manifest itself in a tremble that prevents all attempts to hold the rifle or pistol still. If you can relax your muscles, then there is a sympathetic relaxing of your mental state, the mind becomes quieter, and concentration and muscle control improves.

There are four commonly used ways of breaking the tension which the shooter experiences in a match. These are:

Pause in the execution of the shot

Breathe deeply and with concentration

Move your body or limbs

Take a break from the match

*Pausing.* If you are trying very hard to overcome your nervousness in order to fire the shot but are not having much success, try pausing for a moment, take a few more breaths, allow your concentration to wander slightly and then start the aiming process over again. This could break the tension and enable you to fire the shot cleanly. Too often a shooter endeavours to fire the shot when tensed up only to find that it is a wild shot and may have ruined a run of good shots.

*Breathing.* Breathing is a relaxing process and can aid concentration. It can be done best by coming off aim and resting the weapon. Start concentrating on your breathing, take deeper breaths and concentrate on how you feel as you breathe in, feel yourself pause, feel yourself breathing out and then feel yourself pause again. A good method is to concentrate on breathing in deeply with the abdomen. When inflated, allow the chest to expand to complete the breath, concentrating on the chest expansion. Hold for a few seconds whilst it is comfortable. Slowly breathe out and concentrate on the feel. When you have emptied your lungs pause for a few seconds and then repeat the exercise. Carry out these exercises for at least a minute or until one feels the mental tension is reduced to an acceptable level and you are relaxed.

A good exercise whilst in the shooting position is to take a few 'belly breaths'. Just breathe in with the belly allowing it to expand until it feels like a football, then slowly breathe out. Doing this a few times generally produces an immediate reduction in tension and one can carry on shooting.

*Movement.* Motion can also reduce tension. Bending the knees, walking, taking a few steps, raising on one's toes, in fact any movement can help.

*Taking a break.* If you feel very nervous (extreme match nerves) in the middle of a shoot, the best thing you can do is to take a break, and leave the firing point, if possible away from the range, for a short period until you begin to calm down. It will also help to calm down if specific relaxation exercises are practised.

### RELAXATION METHODS

The most common method of relaxing is to concentrate on relaxing each set of muscles starting with the toes and feet and gradually working up through the legs, stomach, shoulders, arms and finally the face muscles. When you have completed this exercise, you should feel very relaxed!

Another method is called dynamic relaxation. This can be done when you are walking to the range as a preliminary preparation for the match. As you walk, take note of the tension in all the groups of muscles in your body and limbs. Then gradually increase the tension counting up to ten. Next, start relaxing the muscles until you become unsteady on your feet. Now increase the tension slightly to steady the position and keep it there with no further increase in tension. Walking becomes that little bit more relaxed as there are no knotted or tensed muscles beyond those which are necessary to walk efficiently. This relaxation can carry through onto the range, and if necessary the same exercise can be beneficial when on the firing point.

The least that any form of relaxation exercise will do is to take your mind off the worrying aspect and should give you a calmer outlook on the match.

## MENTAL REHEARSAL

Mental rehearsal, or 'imagery' as it is sometimes known, is the process of thinking through the act of shooting without any physical involvement. It is best done after a session of relaxation exercises whilst the mind is in a relaxed, receptive condition. Probably everyone has unknowingly done some mental imagery in his lifetime − thinking about things like a visit to the dentist where we imagine getting into the chair and can visualise what the dentist is going to do, is a form of mental rehearsal. A more positive example is, before going to see our boss about a problem, we imagine what we are going to do and say at the meeting.

Some shooters have seemingly better imaginations than others and can mentally rehearse the whole act of shooting, starting with going to the range, setting out all the equipment, getting into position and then firing each shot, one by one. This of course can take a long time and it is probably better only to attempt specific tasks during a mental training session, such as the firing of a single shot.

To take advantage of mental rehearsal it is essential that the shooter can shoot reasonably well in the first place as it is only beneficial if the procedure rehearsed is a proper one. What we try to do in imagery is to imagine the correct procedures of holding, aiming, trigger release, etc, to reinforce the skills we have learned in actual shooting. What we must not do is rehearse incorrect skills as this would be detrimental to our performance.

It is sometimes of benefit to carry out a short period of mental rehearsal just prior to a match, or even during a match, if problems arise. Its main advantage at those times is that it helps to focus concentration on the shooting and excludes extraneous thought that might cause problems during the match. For example, imagining the act of holding the weapon, would mean mentally going through all the sets of muscles which contribute to holding it steady, which would either reinforce the physical hold or make you suddenly aware that a mistake had been made during previous shots which could then be corrected for the rest of the shoot.

Mental rehearsal after the shoot is useful as one can mentally go through various techniques or changes to techniques that were found to be beneficial and hence those techniques would be reinforced in the mind for the next training session or match. An entry into your shooting diary would also reinforce any changes or new techniques used, and also any possible benefits noticed from mental rehearsal.

Another use of imagery is to desensitise yourself to specific situations. For instance, if there is a member of your club whose presence annoys you or causes nervous tension which would degrade your performance, try visualising the situation many times and endeavour not to be affected by him. By the time you have imagined this several times a day for several weeks you should have overcome, to a large extent, his (or her) effect on your performance. This is desensitisation. The same technique may be useful to desensitise yourself to match pressure. How long it takes to accomplish a satisfactory level of sensitiveness to these situations does depend to a large extent on the individual's personal make up and motivation, but it is another ploy to try, to enable you to shoot your training scores, or higher, under match conditions.

AUTOGENIC TRAINING (AT)

Autogenic training is a relatively recent introduction into sport in Britain although athletes in Europe and elsewhere have been doing it for some time. It is a scientific and systematic western form of meditation intended to allow the power or suggestion to influence the body.

In shooting it is the mental control that probably has the most effect on whether a shooter can succeed in competitions. It is not only competitions where mental control is essential but even in practice where he may be heading for a good practice score or group and loss of mental control suddenly ruins his performance in the final few shots. We have all experienced this effect and the same happens in many other sports. AT has been used successfully by many prominent athletes and shooters to overcome this effect and to keep performance consistent throughout the competition. Even those who are only interested in sporting airgun shooting will benefit from learning AT as it is a means of being able to withstand discomforts such as cold and having to stay in position for lengthy periods if stalking game.

The originator of AT was Dr J. H. Schultz who died at the age of eighty-six in 1970. Dr Schultz noted in his research that people under hypnosis experience two effects: a peculiar heaviness and warmth in the limbs. Hypnosis induces a sort of mental change and the feelings of heaviness and warmth occur in connection with this change. AT also produces this feeling of heaviness and warmth and when this is achieved the person can be said to be in a state of autogenic relaxation.

Only a systematic procedure will develop the full effects of AT and the beginner should follow the instructions as closely as possible. It is preferable to find a psychologist or other instructor who can teach AT and it is useful to do it as a group under his instruction. Shooters who live within a reasonable distance of London should contact the Autogenic Training Centre where this new system is taught. However, as it is a new technique, many shooters will be unable to find such a person and they will have to resort to being self-taught. It is beyond the scope of this book to give adequate information on the method but a book, *Relieve Tension the Autogenic Way*, has been written by Hannes Lindemann who used Autogenics to help survive his single handed crossing of the Atlantic by canoe.

### Diet

To my knowledge there has been very little work, if any, carried out on research into the optimum diet for a shooter. Undoubtedly there are some foods which can effect individual people but it is difficult to generalise and recommend a diet which would be suitable for all shooters.

It is recognised that coffee, tea and Coca Cola contain the

stimulant caffeine which affects the pulse rate, and in general these drinks should not be taken close to the time of the match. However, it is also a mistake to avoid these drinks altogether when the match approaches because there could be withdrawal symptoms which are equally bad, if not worse. Unfortunately, it is not even possible to state that these drinks do affect your shooting because their main effect is to increase the pulse rate slightly, but one can still shoot well with an increased rate providing it is not too high already. If the match is one which is likely to create considerable match pressure and hence a significant pulse rate increase, it would be foolhardy to drink or eat anything which will increase the pulse rate any further unless it has a beneficial effect in calming you down. As can be seen, this is a very personal judgement and one that require's experiment to find out how it effects you.

During training and through most of the year, you can eat what you want. The time when a little more thought should be addressed to food and drink is in the final stages of training or just prior to a big match. If you find some food or drink that does have a detrimental affect on your scores, make a note of it so that it can be avoided before the match. It is advisable to avoid heavy meals within a couple of hours of the match or training, as the discomfort of a full stomach will distract your concentration during the shoot and a higher than normal pulse rate will occur. Food that is eaten should be an easily digestible variety.

Breakfast is an important meal of the day and should not be avoided even when you have an early morning match. Make sure you get up early enough to have a reasonable breakfast such as fruit juices, cereals, toast or bread rolls with jam or honey. If you miss breakfast, you may feel a bit weak during the match and will not be able to give the match your full concentration.

In general, you should not eat or drink during the match but, if the match is difficult and the range is hot, or cold, then the benefit of a small cool drink or a sip of weak tea or chocolate would outweigh the disadvantages.

Try to avoid changes in style of food when shooting away at matches. This is not easy as the food, even in a British Hotel, will be different from what you eat at home, and if you are shooting abroad, the food may be very different and there is always the added temptation of trying new foods. The least you can do is to try to have normal foods before the match unless you have acclimatised to the type of food by arriving a week or more before the match.

## Drugs

Drugs are used in all types of sport, to increase strength, reduce tiredness and suppress pain or inhibitions. Most drugs are taken to increase the athlete's performance beyond what he is normally capable of achieving by normal training methods. In shooting most of these drugs are unnecessary and often have a detrimental rather than beneficial effect. Because shooting is improved more by mental attitudes than physical prowess, those drugs which increase strength or endurance are of no use because there are mental or physical side effects. These effects are usually a loss of the fine control of muscle tensions, co-ordination and reactions which are an absolute necessity in top-class shooting performance.

Drugs which are tranquillisers would help to calm the shooter's nerves but, again, would have the side effects of lack of fine control and almost an attitude of indifference to the match. This might improve the nervous shooter who is a mental wreck when shooting in matches but it would certainly not improve his scores above what he is normally capable of achieving in training and is more likely to reduce his performance compared with what he might achieve by a mental training programme. Sedatives the night before the match may help the agitated shooter to sleep but there is always the possibility that the effect may not have worn off completely, prior to the match.

It is often difficult to avoid taking drugs as many of our popular drinks are, or contain, drugs. Although coffee and tea contain caffeine, the beneficial effect of a cup of tea under certain conditions far outweigh the side effects. Possibly a different drink such as hot chocolate may be acceptable as a substitute for tea or coffee on the day of the match.

Alcohol is a drug yet some countries traditionally drink wine at mealtimes. Small amounts would be beneficial to shooters who are accustomed to drinking it regularly so are we right to class it as a drug and ban its use in shooting, when to do so would penalise those countries where it is taken regularly. Checks are sometimes made but these are really concerned with safety, as an excess of alcohol taken by a shooter might make him a hazard on the range. However, it is generally agreed that alcohol should not be taken by the shooter on the day of the match. Also if taken in large quantities the night before, it would have a detrimental effect on performance.

Pep pills may be alright for some more dynamic sports but the loss of fine co-ordination which occurs rules out its use for shooting. Beta Blockers are a new drug which depress the beta waves from the brain and suppress the flow of adrenalin which can increase during a match. However, although they do appear to have a beneficial effect on nervous shooters, they do not give the top shooter who has trained effectively any advantage and could limit his performance by dulling the 'killer streak' which often gives the winner an advantage over a less aggressive shooter.

Cigarettes contain nicotine which is an addictive drug. A smoker's physiology depends upon the level of nicotine in the bloodstream and if he stops smoking he will experience withdrawal symptoms. Smoking is harmful to health and even smokers who exercise suffer from the effects of the drug. Those who smoke regularly and cannot break the habit should not attempt to stop smoking before the match because the withdrawal symptoms would harm his performance. Those who despise the use of drugs in sport should remember that cigarettes contain the drug nicotine which gives a calming effect to the shooter and which is not really any different from taking a tranquilliser drug.

The conclusion is that, although drugs may make one feel better, there is no evidence to suggest that a drug can improve one's shooting ability. As drugs are banned under Olympic rules, it is also wiser for the up and coming shooter not to use drugs, even if he finds them beneficial, but to try, through training, to achieve the same result.

# 10 Training Programmes

The majority of shooters throughout the world are club shooters who would like to aspire to nothing greater than being club champion. There are a relatively few shooters who set their sights on becoming a World or Olympic Champion.

The most efficient method of achieving both of these aspirations is to prepare a training programme. Without some form of plan you may not achieve either aim and hence this chapter is intended to give some idea of what is involved. A training plan can cover several years or it may be only one year. The plan should be aimed at a particular event to give a focus for training, and the higher the event the greater must be the effort; also the longer, more thorough and meticulous must be the training programme as the winner will be the one who has overcome all the physical and mental barriers necessary to produce the winning performance.

The object of training should be to improve performance. If you can improve performance, then the scores will look after themselves. It is better to concentrate on performance and not to concern yourself too much with achieving scores. Scores are an indicator of performance and will be useful in assessing whether a sufficient rate of improvement is being made in order to reach your ultimate goal. When setting a goal score, you should not be constrained by making it a specific score but rather by making it not less than a specific score. In other words to set a target of 580 by a certain date would be setting a limit on your possible achievement, whereas setting a *minimum* goal of achieving at least 580 would not create such a barrier to be overcome; scores in excess of this would be expected and you would be more likely to achieve 580 or even higher.

It is useful to set intermediate goals through the training period. These could be minimum scores to achieve by certain dates. They act as a focus for your efforts although the object is primarily to improve performance rather than be constrained by scores. Realistic goals should be set, otherwise concentration will be directed to scores when you should be concentrating on improving the individual elements of hold, aim, trigger release and mental aspects.

In setting the ultimate goal you can try and predict the minimum score which should win the competition and select this as your minimum aim. However, you must also be realistic and try to estimate the scores which you should be capable of shooting at the completion of your training plan. For instance, a beginner should not try to use as his goal a score which would win the National Championship when that championship is only six months away. With the time that he is able to devote to training, he should try to estimate how much improvement in performance he could make in that time and set the target score accordingly. He may not win the Championship with that score, but if he can achieve his target score in the competition then he would have confidence in his training plan and could then produce a plan which would enable him to achieve the winning score perhaps next time.

Choosing your target score is not easy as you may have very little idea of what rate of progress to expect so you should not endeavour to set your aims too high or you may be discouraged. You must decide how many hours can be devoted to training, make out a plan covering the period to the chosen event and realistically decide on the basis of the plan how much progress could be made and the minimum score you believe you can achieve.

An essential part of training is to shoot in matches. If you have chosen a particular match as the goal, then all preceding matches can be called training matches. Training matches are essential as they give the opportunity to put everything you have learnt beforehand to the test of durability under match pressures. The holds you have developed, the trigger technique and, above all, the usefulness of any mental training can be evaluated under match conditions. Each match you shoot adds to your knowledge and mental control so that at the end of the training programme, you are as ready as you can be for the final match.

Where possible, matches should be chosen so that they gradually become harder. In this way your techniques can be carefully improved and you would build up success. If a difficult match was chosen as a starter you would be mentally resigned to losing and you could not really put your techniques to the test. Far better to choose one which would make you try very hard but was within your ability to win. You would then taste success and if you increase the difficulty with each match, you would be testing your improvement in performance as it builds up to the final match.

Unfortunately, it is not always easy to choose matches of the appropriate levels because matches are not held at regular intervals through the season, and they can be very widely separated. In Britain, for instance, there are, at the time of writing, a number of good matches during August to November which are very useful as training for our National Championship at Cardiff in October. However, between November and February there are virtually no matches which can be used as training for the European Championships held in February. Because of the increasing interest in air rifle and pistol shooting, this is likely to change but there will always be areas of the country where there will be a shortage of suitable matches. In these cases the shooter must be prepared to travel extensively.

Having decided the ultimate goal, which could be, say, to become National Champion or even Olympic Champion in four years time, you make out intermediate goals to achieve during the intervening years. These intermediate goals could be to become Club Champion as a first goal, then County Champion as the second goal, Area Champion as third goal and National Champion as the ultimate goal.

| Year | 1 | 2 | 3 | 4 |
|---|---|---|---|---|
| Match | Club Champ | County Champ | Regional Champ | British Champ |
| Min train sc. | 550 | 560 | 570 | 578 |
| Min match sc. | 540 | 555 | 565 | 575 |

| Year | 1 | 2 | 3 | 4 |
|---|---|---|---|---|
| Match | British Champ | Nordic Champ | European Champ | World Champ |
| Min train sc. | 578 | 583 | 585 | 587 |
| Min match sc. | 575 | 580 | 583 | 585 |

93 Typical four year training plans

| Month | 1st Qtr | | | 2nd Qtr | | | 3rd Qtr | | | 4th Qtr | | |
|---|---|---|---|---|---|---|---|---|---|---|---|---|
| | 1 | 2 | 3 | 1 | 2 | 3 | 1 | 2 | 3 | 1 | 2 | 3 |
| Min. Tr. Sc. | 565 | | | 570 | | | 575 | | | 579 | | |
| Min. Mat. Sc. | | | | | | 570 | | | 575 | | | 579 |

Min. Tr. Sc.   Predicted minimum training score to be acheived in that period
Min. Mat. Sc.  Predicted minimum match score to be acheived in that period at selected matches

94 Typical yearly performance plan

| Date | Physical | | Mental | | Shots to fire | | | | | Prac. | | Match | | | | Notes |
|---|---|---|---|---|---|---|---|---|---|---|---|---|---|---|---|---|
| | 5BX | Run | AT | Reh | 20 | 40 | 60 | 80 | 100 | Gr | Sep. | Club | Coun | Op | Tl | |
| Mar 1 | ✓ | ✓ | | | ✓ | | | | | | ✓ | | | | | |
| 2 | | | ✓ | | | ✓ | | | | ✓ | | | | | | |
| 3 | ✓ | ✓ | | | | | | | | | | | | | | |
| 4 | | | ✓ | ✓ | | | | | | | | | | | | |
| 5 | ✓ | ✓ | | | ✓ | | | | | | | ✓ | | | | |
| 6 | | | ✓ | | | | | | | | | | | | | |
| 7 | ✓ | ✓ | | | | | | | | | | | | | | |
| Jan 1 | ✓ | ✓ | ✓ | | | ✓ | | | | | ✓ | | | | | |
| 2 | | | | ✓ | | ✓ | | | | | | ✓ | | | | |
| 3 | ✓ | ✓ | ✓ | | | | ✓ | | | | ✓ | | | | | |
| 4 | | | | | ✓ | | | | | ✓ | | | | | | |
| 5 | ✓ | ✓ | ✓ | ✓ | | | | | | | | | | | | |
| 6 | | | | | | | ✓ | | | | | | | ✓ | | |
| 7 | | | ✓ | | | | | ✓ | | | | | ✓ | | | |

AT  Autogenic training    Club Club matches
Reh Mental rehearsal      Coun. County matches
Gr  Grouping            Op  Open matches
Sep Separate diagrams     Tr  Trials

95 Extract from a typical training calendar

An overall plan for the four year period can be drawn up based on the selected ultimate and intermediate goals. Two plans for shooters of different ability are shown in Fig 93. Detailed plans can then be drawn up for the first year on a day-by-day basis. Minimum performances at the end of each week or month should be predicted and can be used to check rate of progress (Fig 94). A special training calendar (Fig 95) should be kept for the plan, giving details of the programme so that the shooter can constantly refer to it. Unless the programme is written up on a calendar basis there will be an uneven rate of progress, as there will be a temptation to do very little at the beginning of a training period and too much towards the end of a period in order to try to achieve the goal. Keep the programme in a prominent place so that you don't lose it or, for that matter, avoid it. Keep a copy at your bedside to encourage you to do the physical and mental training when you arise or before bed. Keep a copy at work to remind you of what you are going to do in the evening when you return from work and also at lunchtimes. The programme should commence with general fitness training, then evolve into general and special fitness training, dry/live firing, live firing and then preliminary matches leading to the big match. Individual training plans must, of course, be based on the shooter's own aspirations and time available.

The two separate match seasons make a training programme difficult to organise. This is another reason why it is essential to make a programme so that one can fit in the physical training, shooting training and competition training in the correct sequences to win the goal for that year.

The training plan is aimed at producing improvements in the performance of the shooter to enable him to win a particular event so all the interim aims are based on individual performances. Many training plans exclude league shooting because the shooter should be concentrating on improving performance rather than scores during the early part of the programme. If you are shooting in a team taking part in a league, the concentration would be on scores and it is likely that these would not improve much through the season compared to those which would be achieved by concentrating on performance. If leagues are to be shot, then you should keep the number to a minimum so that sufficient time is left for performance training.

As you will have noticed in this chapter, a lot of emphasis is put on performance. Performance training is looking at each part of the act of shooting – hold, aiming, trigger release, follow through, and concentration on each one to try to improve it. The improvement will also give beneficial results in the integrated act of shooting and scores will improve through performance improvement and not through concentrating on achieving scores. Unlike most sports, the shooter is almost in a world of his own when competing against others as he does not know how well they are performing and whether they are better than he, so his entire concentration must go into producing a faultless performance. Whether he wins or not depends on how well he puts all the separate elements of the integrated act of shooting together, how well he performs each act, whether his goal score was high enough to win and whether he achieved that score. As he cannot do anything to alter his opponents' performance his entire concentration should be devoted to his own performance.

THE SHOOTER'S DIARY

From the time you decide that you want to improve your performance and write your training programme, you should commence your shooting diary. A shooter's diary is a record of what he has done each day throughout the programme:

## SAT. 11th MARCH

Arrived at range after difficult time in traffic jam. Decided to settle down for 45 minutes before shooting. Started at 2.45. Used FWB 300SU and H&N pellets (500 box). Took 15 minutes over 5 sighters then started match. Hold a little twitchy and kept flicking shots out to 2.0 o'clock. Sat down after first 10 match shots. Returned to position and found that hold was much better, so must have had bad position on first 10. Group was central. Finished 40 shots with 10 sighters in 1 hour 15 minutes. Score was 45, 48, 48, 48, 49, 47, 49 381. Shot one 8 in first 5 shots then all 9's and 10's. Noticed that I had to adjust sights 3 clicks right and 2 high for some reason. Must check to see if it happens next time.

It should outline your programme for the day and, after each activity, you should record what you did, the results of any changes, the score achieved, the reasons for good or bad performances, the weather, time, weapon used, ammunition used, how you felt physically and mentally, what exercises were carried out, any problems and what if anything you should do the next day if it is not already included in the programme. Throughout the programme, changes in techniques and equipment will be made and, unless a record is kept, the effect of each change will be lost. This becomes increasingly important as the diary grows because you can refer back several weeks or months to check up on different changes. You can also make changes with confidence, knowing that you can go back to the exact position or configuration as before the change. Record everything! It is even worthwhile recording what you eat, how well you slept, what work you did and other personal aspects.

BEFORE THE MATCH

In the last few weeks before the match no changes to position or equipment should be made. All changes should have been done earlier and now is the period for consolidation of the techniques which have been found to be most beneficial to your performance. The training sessions should be at least as long as the match period and preferably with some extra time in the build up training sessions. Concentration must remain on performance but the scores can now be noted as genuine indications of the levels of performance reached. This also gets the mind conditioned to achieving high scores. Mental training is all important now as this is the item which determines whether you shoot to your training standard in the match or whether you let the match affect you and you do not reach the standard of performance for which you had trained.

The equipment should all be functioning correctly with particular emphasis on ensuring that the weapon and its pellets have been tested together and are giving good groups.

It is no good training yourself up to peak performance if you are going to lose points through using pellets which cannot produce small groups. The tighter the group capability, the more errors in performance we can make and yet still hit the 10 ring.

All looseness in the sights and the attachment screws should be removed well before the match so that on the day there will be complete confidence in the equipment. Many points have been lost through sights coming loose from the weapon.

Personal activities should be those which you may have found gave you an improved performance in training or at least was not detrimental to your performance. These include what food you had eaten and the interval between eating and shooting. Did going to bed early help or was it better to go late so that you would fall asleep quickly and not be kept awake worrying about the match.

# 11 Competitions

Competitive air rifle and pistol shooting is a well-organised sport both nationally and internationally. Because of the simplicity of setting up an airweapon range and the cheapness of shooting, the growth of the sport is ensured as the costs of other target shooting sports such as small bore and full bore shooting are caught up in the inflationary spiral. Having bought the airgun and shooting jacket, the cost of pellets is negligible and one can shoot for a year at a cost of only a few pounds.

As the sport grows, there will be a growth in competitions and already many counties organise their own leagues and have their own championships. The National Small-Bore Rifle Association also organise nationwide leagues and competitions for clubs and county teams, and competitions for individual shooters.

## Postal Competitions

The majority of competitions both for teams and individual shooters are organised on a postal basis. In postal competitions, the competitors shoot their targets on their own ranges but within specified time-scales and dates. Clubs or counties select their teams and submit their averages to the organisers who then, in the case of leagues, organise the teams into a number of divisions consisting of up to, say, ten teams. Each team would then shoot their targets on their home range and send the shot targets to the scorer. The teams shoot against one another as in a football league, but the team does not know whether it has won a match until the scorer has scored both teams and the scores are compared.

The results are then posted back to the clubs involved. The scorers are chosen by the organisers of the league and are not normally connected with any of the teams shooting in the division for which he has responsibility. This is to ensure fairness in scoring.

The league tables are then drawn up as shown in the table below, which is similar to most other sports' league table systems.

| Team | S | W | D | L | P | Agg |
|------|---|---|---|---|---|-----|
| Team A | | | | | | |
| Team B | | | | | | |
| Team C | | | | | | |
| Team D | | | | | | |
| etc | | | | | | |

**S** = No. of matches shot
**W** = No. of matches won
**D** = No. of matches drawn
**L** = No. of matches lost
**P** = Total points on the basis of 2 for a win, 1 for a draw, and 0 for losing
**Agg** = Aggregate. This is the total score of the team in all matches to date

Individual leagues are organised on the same basis as team leagues, and in the above table the team column would consist of individuals' names.

An essential part of postal shooting is witnessing. A shooter is not allowed to shoot in a postal match unless an authorised witness is present to ensure that the rules of the competition are adhered to when he shoots his targets. The targets are either provided by the organisers and bear official identification or special adhesive labels are attached to the targets before they are shot. Unless the rules are enforced and witnessing carried out fairly, the postal system would not work. In Britain, the system works well and there are very few cases brought before the organising bodies for discipline.

In any case there is no real satisfaction in winning a match by cheating and, because there is very little commercialism in the sport, the remuneration is not really worth the risk as the penalty could be disqualification from all competitions.


**Shoulder-to-Shoulder Competitions**

Clubs, counties and the national organising bodies also run shoulder-to-shoulder competitions in which the competitors gather together at a specific range and compete side by side. Because of the number of competitors who enter these matches, the facilities must be large and, for a national or county competition, up to 100 firing points may be involved.

In consequence, many organisers hire sports halls and fit automatic target changers (which can also be hired) so that the competition can be held over a weekend to accommodate the large number of shooters expected. County organisers have held competitions for several hundred shooters in this way very successfully.

Competitive shooting in Britain is well organised and competitions are open to all levels of proficiency. Matches which are for individual shooters, rather than teams, are often graded into classes ranging from A to E. Each class apart from A Class can only be entered by competitors whose average does not exceed the stated average. The competitions organised by the National Small-Bore Rifle Association have classes with the following averages:

|  | Rifle | Pistol |
|---|---|---|
| Class A over | 88.5 | 90 |
| Class B over | 84.5 and under 88.5 | 86 and under 90 |
| Class C under | 84.5 | 86 |

The averages submitted must be provided by the competitor's club and be verified by the club secretary or captain. This ensures that all competitors have a fair chance of winning an award in their own class.

Most other organisations set their own classification averages which are not always the same as the national body. A common method of establishing classes is to ask all competitors when submitting an entry to state their current average as verified by the club secretary or captain. The averages are then taken and classes are established so that there is an equal number of competitors in each class based on their averages.

Competitions are usually advertised in one of the shooting journals and details and entry forms are sent to those clubs and individuals who are interested. Having received details, the interested party fills in the entry form with personal details such as name and address, the competitions to be entered, his certified average, the time he wishes to shoot and sends it off to the organiser along with a cheque for entry fees. There is usually a closing date for entries and the organiser will await the closing date before allocating competitors to the squads and firing points that are available. He will then write to the clubs or individuals and inform them of the allocated time, firing point, and competitors number.

On arrival at the venue of the match, the competitor goes to the weapon control, or stats (statistics) table where he will be asked for his competition number and will have his rifle or pistol checked to ensure that it complies with the rules. His other equipment such as shooting jacket and boots may also be checked. All equipment must comply with the rules so ensure that you are aware of them and that your equipment is within these rules before you arrive at the match. Otherwise you will be requested to change those items not satisfying the rules or you would not be allowed to take part in the competition. Having passed the checks you will be given your set of targets for the competition. Sometimes adhesive labels are given bearing identification of the competition and competitor which must be stuck on the targets before firing.

As these checks and the issue of targets does take time, you are advised to arrive at the venue well ahead of the hour for your squad so that time can be spent on relaxing, getting the right mental attitude, acclimatising yourself to the temperature and shooting environment and preparing your equipment. If you are the sort of person who has a fierce competitive nature, you might take advantage from looking at the score sheets which are hung up in the scoring or stats area. This can give you some idea of how good the competition is but it shouldn't really be necessary if you have trained yourself to win the match by setting a minimum score to be achieved at that match. Most successful shooters do not look at the scores until after they have shot as it may make them more nervous when the scores they must beat are seen.

When the time comes to set yourself up on the nominated firing point do so without rushing and position everything (pellets, timer, targets and telescope) as if it were a training shoot. Ensure that you know the range orders, the time allowed and target changing procedures. If possible be on the firing point at least 15 minutes before the match commences so that your equipment can be made ready and do some dry firing so as to get your muscles and co-ordination functioning efficiently before the match starts. It is surprising how many changes in feel and hold occur during the start of shooting. Consequently dry firing may eliminate the need for sight changes once the match starts. In any case most shooters are unsteady when picking up the weapon for the first few shots and steadiness gradually improves with each shot whether dry or live.

The range officer usually allows time for warming up shots to be fired. This is so that the mechanisms can be operated to overcome any stickiness which might have occurred due to lack of use for a period, and also to foul the barrel if it has been cleaned. These warming up shots are fired at the bullet trap without a target being there.

When the order is given to fire the target is sent up to the end of the range by using the automatic target changer, if the range is fortunate enough to be equipped with them. If automatic target changers are not being used, it is unlikely that you would be allowed warming up shots because of the inconvenience of having to walk up and place the targets at the butts. The competition rules will indicate how many sighting shots are allowed, and whether they are to be fired at the beginning of the competition or can be fired between strings of 10 shots throughout the match. Do not fire more sighters than allowed. It should also be noted that you do not need to fire all your sighters before commencing the match but can start the match when you are satisfied with the sighters. Competitions allow either one or two shots per diagram for rifle shooting and between one and five shots per target for pistol.

As the match targets are completed they should be given to the range officer, placed in the target receptacle, on the chair behind or kept until all the targets have been shot as dictated by the competition rules. The targets are collected and sent to the 'statistics' for scoring. When the targets are scored and checked, the score is entered on the score sheets which are displayed in a location where the shooters can see everyone's score. If the shooter does not agree with the score he can challenge it and have his targets rechecked. There is usually a nominal fee to be paid for this which is returned if the challenge is successful, otherwise the fee is forfeited. The idea, of course, is to prevent people challenging unless they are convinced the score was marked wrongly. Usually the cause of the challenge is when one of the shots fired is a 'squeaker' and it becomes necessary to use a scoring gauge to determine whether the shot has touched the higher scoring ring or not. A scoring gauge is a specially designed flanged plug which fits into the shot hole. Depending on whether it is an inward or outward scoring gauge the flange should either touch the higher scoring ring or one of the lower scoring rings respectively. The inward scoring gauge need only just touch the higher ring in order to be awarded the higher score, whereas with the outward gauge the flange must not completely cross the appropriate lower ring in order to be awarded the higher value for the shot.

In international competitions all squeakers are gauged automatically and, if a challenge is made, they cannot be regauged because the act of gauging can enlarge the hole. Such challenges can thus only be made regarding the score as indicated on the scoreboards — if a mistake had been made in entering the score, the challenge would be upheld.

Ties are decided by a standard procedure contained in the rules. The first three places under UIT rules are decided by

1   The highest number of 10s, 9s, 8s, 7s etc. If the tie cannot be decided by this method then
2   The highest number of inner 10s (an inner 10 is when the white 10 dot is completely obscured) on the rifle target

If any ties remain the awards will be duplicated. Ties in team competitions are decided by the same method.

Prizes are awarded to each class and these depend on the number of entries, the cost of running the competition and the degree of sponsorship obtained. Prizes can be anything from a medal (plate 14) to a new rifle or pistol. If sponsorship has been obtained, it is always good practice to publish the results as widely as possible in order to ensure that the sponsor as well as the sport receives benefit from the publicity.

A point worth bearing in mind is that there are definite rules regarding the amount of prize money allowed to be won in order to remain an amateur and also the degree to which an individual shooter can be sponsored.

## International Shooting

Because of its popularity, shooting is carried on world-wide and has its own international competitions, as explained earlier. Teams and individuals must be selected by the national organising bodies, and for major international championships the selections are agreed, in Britain, by the Joint Shooting Council.

In order to select a team, Britain, like many other

countries, has a National Squad for air rifle and pistol shooting which carries out a training programme throughout the year. This culminates in a series of selection trials in order to pick the team for the international matches. The National Squad is in two groups: the 'A' Squad consisting nominally of the six top shooters, and the 'B' Squad which contains up to twelve of the next best shooters. The national team is usually selected from the 'A' Squad at the completion of the trials, but if a shooter in the 'B' Squad shows great promise and beats the 'A' Squad members then he may be selected for the team. If an 'A' Squad member fails to become selected for a team over a period of two years, then he may be relegated to the 'B' Squad and a 'B' Squad member takes his place. There are definite advantages in being selected for the 'A' Squad as, in addition to being eligible for the teams, he also gets more financial support for training and is in a better position to apply to organisations like the Sports Aid Foundation for assistance in training.

The National Rifle Squad is an élite squad and entry to the squad is by standard of performance in selected matches and a final selection trial. A number of shoulder-to-shoulder matches can be nominated throughout the country and performance in these matches is noted by the NSRA. The final selection trial is then arranged and the top shooters from the nominated matches are invited to take part. The top shooters in the trial are then invited to join the 'B' Squad to replace those who will be dropped from the squad because of lack of success in making the 'A' Squad within a given period.

The National Pistol Squad is organised on similar lines to the above but with some differences. Anyone interested and shooting to a high enough standard should write to the NSRA for current details of the selection procedure as they are subject to change.

The national squads meet regularly and train together on the firing range. Training programmes are discussed and agreed similar to those discussed in Chapter 10. There are a number of national coaches to help on all shooting problems and their main role is to ensure that the shooter improves his performance until he is good enough to become selected to represent Britain in an international match. Not only that, but they will not be satisfied until that shooter wins a medal (preferably Gold) in these matches. This is the aim of the National Squads, to win international honours, so the shooter must be prepared to sacrifice much of his time to becoming proficient enough to do this. Age is not an insurmountable problem as there are many top class shooters at all ages up to say sixty years. Enthusiasm and perseverence backed up by a good training and analytical ability are what will take you to the top.

Having been selected for the team is not the end of the story. The shooter must keep training to try and lift his scores even higher. No one has scored 600 yet (or 400 ladies and juniors) so don't be satisfied until you do! The team will be informed of all the arrangements being made to get them to the international match which, in Britain, usually means that the team of rifle and pistol shooters will eventually meet at Heathrow or some other airport for the first time. The weapons must all be securely boxed as they travel in the cargo hold and will be very roughly handled (luggage weight should be kept to a minimum because of excess charges).

On arrival at the foreign venue the team is usually met by a representative of that country's organising body. He will smooth the way through customs and help with any language problems. Most major international match organisers arrange to have interpreters with the teams. The team is then taken to the hotel, or to the range to store the weapons.

The team manager and team captain will receive a programme which details the practice sessions and firing points allocated to the team. The captain will then arrange a firing pont and time allowance for each shooter. As range space is very limited it is likely that the shooter would not have the time allowed for a full course so all training should have been done before the team departs from England and these practice sessions are only used just to keep in trim and to become accustomed to the conditions.

There is always an opening ceremony to attend where flags are raised and speeches made. A camera to record the event is a must, particularly for 'first timers'. It is a very formal occasion and most teams are in uniform.

Equipment must be submitted to Weapon Control to ensure that it complies with the rules. It is surprising how many shooters use equipment which does not comply and you will always see someone using a knife or scissors on clothing or a saw or file on their weapon in order to pass the tests. Always check equipment against the rule book during training and don't leave it until you arrive at a match.

You will meet many shooters from other nationalities and despite language differences they will discuss all sorts of topics (including shooting!) and there is always badge swapping taking place, which is a great social barrier breaker. Badge swapping takes place at all international events so it is advisable to ensure that an adequate supply of NSRA, ESSU, NARPA and other badges are available for this purpose.

Before the day of the match the team captain will give out firing point numbers, timings, range procedures and competitors' numbers. A discussion will also take place on the amount of team support to be provided for each shooter. Some shooters like someone they know sitting behind them throughout the match, others prefer no one. However, it is essential to know that help is available should one need it as often there are difficulties during the match which are best sorted out by the team captain or manager so as to leave the shooter to concentrate solely on shooting performance. Also, if he gets into difficulties during the match, he can leave the firing point and go in amongst the spectators for a change, or advice. No advice is allowed on the firing point so the shooter must ensure that he has left it before talking to anyone but range officials.

Each shooter may also have a scorer sitting directly behind him estimating his score and writing it on a score sheet which is displayed to spectators. It must be remembered that these are only estimated scores and are often done by non-shooters, even children from local schools, so the shooter should not pin his hopes or disappointments on these scores. The official scores are displayed on a scoreboard outside the range area and these are the final scores, unless a successful challenge is made.

At the end of the match he will feel elated, or depressed, depending on his score. He can then leave the range and have some refreshments to celebrate or drown his sorrows. However, he should make sure he has checked his score on the official scoreboard before going back to the hotel because mistakes can be made and they must be corrected as soon as possible.

Medal awards take place before the closing ceremony and are formal affairs with the national anthem of each winner being played whilst his national flag is raised. An official banquet often takes place at the closing of the match where a lot of friends are made and usually the parties carry on in team rooms afterwards.

# Further Reading

Antal, Lazlo *Pistol Shooting* (KTG-EP Publishing, 1981)
Cooper, Kenneth *The New Aerobics* (Bantam, 1970)
Klinger, Bernd *Rifle Shooting as a Sport* (Kaye & Ward, 1980)
Morehouse, Laurence E. and Gross, Leonard *Maximum Performance* (Mayflower, 1980)
Pullum, Bill and Hanenkrat, Frank T. *Position Rifle Shooting* (Winchester Press, 1973)
Royal Canadian Air Force *Physical Fitness* (Penguin, 1970)
Standl, Hans *Pistol Shooting as a Sport* (Kaye & Ward, 1975)

*Airgun World* Monthly magazine devoted to all airweapon shooting, including field and target shooting
*Guns Review* Monthly magazine for firearms and airweapon enthusiasts
*The Rifleman* Bimonthly NSRA magazine concerned with target shooting using airweapons and firearms
*Target Gun* Monthly magazine devoted to all target shooting sports
*UIT International Shooting Sport* Bimonthly magazine for target shooters interested in international shooting aspects

# Useful Addresses

National Small-Bore Rifle Association
Lord Roberts House
Bisley Camp
Brockwood
Surrey
GU24 0NP

National Air Rifle and Pistol Association
44 High Street
Bridgnorth
Shropshire
WV16 4DX

The Autogenic Training Centre
14a Milford House
7 Queen Anne Street
London W1M 9FD

# Acknowledgements

In the course of writing any book, many people contribute to the author's store of knowledge, and while it is impossible to list all the individuals who have helped us, to the following we are especially grateful: the National Small-Bore Rifle Association for permission to use their badge and targets within the text; the National Air Rifle & Pistol Association for similar permission; Frank Dyke & Co for permission to use drawings from the 'Original' catalogue; Accuracy International, ASI Ltd, BSA Ltd, Webley & Scott Ltd and Parker Hale Ltd for information on their various products; Chris Potter Guns Ltd and the London Airgun Centre for facilities to test airweapons; and to M. Baxter, Mrs J. Carter and Mrs J. Coleman for their advice and assistance.

# Index